The Natural History Society of Jamaica

The Natural History Society of Jamaica

Guide to the Blue & John Crow Mountains

Edited by Margaret Hodges

First published in Jamaica 2008,
for and on behalf of the Natural History Society of Jamaica by
Ian Randle Publishers
11 Cunningham Avenue
Box 686
Kingston 6
www.ianrandlepublishers.com

© 2008, The Natural History Society of Jamaica
All Rights Reserved. Published 2008

Funded by The Environmental Foundation of Jamaica

National Library of Jamaica Cataloguing in Publication Data

The Natural History Society of Jamaica: Guide to the Blue and John Crow Mountains / edited by Margaret Hodges.

p. : ill., maps ;   cm.

ISBN 978-976-637-269-9

1. Natural history – Jamaica. 2. Jamaica – Description and travel. 3. Mountains - Jamaica

I. Hodges, Margaret.

508.7292   dc 21

All rights reserved. No part of this publication may be reproduced, stored in a retrieval system, or transmitted in any form, or by any means electronic, photocopying, recording or otherwise without the prior permission of the Natural History Society of Jamaica or publisher.

Cover photo by Stephen Hodges
Cover and book design by Ian Randle
Printed in China by Regent Publishing Services Ltd

CONTENTS

Acknowledgements..vii

Introduction..ix
Robert Kerr

Travelling in the Mountains...1
Margaret Hodges

The Park and Its Surroundings, with local maps......................8
Jill Byles and Margaret Hodges
Maps by Stephen Hodges

The Western Section 9

Approaches to the Blue Mountains from
Kingston and St. Andrew...23

The Southern Approaches: The Blue Mountains
Foothills from St. Thomas...71

The Eastern Section..79

The Eastern Slopes of the John Crow Mountains....................85

The Rio Grande Valley..101

The Northern Section..112

The Historical Background...125
Mary Langford

The Geology..134
Ryan Ramsook

The Flora..140
Jim Dalling and Margaret Hodges

The Fungi...155
Trevor Yee

The Invertebrates...161
Eric Garraway and Audette Bailey

The Vertebrates..170
Thomas Farr

The Birds of the Mountain Area...................................176
Catherine Levy and Marcia Mundle

Life in Streams and Rivers...189
Kimberly John and Eric Hyslop

Appendix...194

ACKNOWLEDGEMENTS

Many members and friends of the Natural History Society have contributed to this book, intended as a guide to Jamaica's first terrestrial national park, the Blue and John Crow Mountains Park.

Much of the information from a previous publication, now out of print, has been included, for which I thank the authors: Paul Steege, Jill Byles, Mary Langford, Dr Rafi Amad, Dr Jim Dalling, Dr Eric Garraway and Catherine Levy. Dr Thomas Farr's contribution on vertebrates has also been included; unfortunately, Dr Farr died in 1996.

© S. HODGES

My thanks to the writers of the new guide go to Robert Kerr, one of the founders of the park, for his introduction; to Mary Langford for a complete rewrite of the history; to Ryan Ramsook for the geology; to Dr George Proctor, eminent botanist, who kindly made suggestions and corrections to the botany of the John Crow section – any mistakes are mine; and to Dr Trevor Yee, who introduced and photographed fungi. Thanks also to Dr Audette Bailey for her section on the invertebrates commonly found in the John Crows and for her help with photographs, and Dr Marcia Mundle, who added notes on the relevant birds. Many thanks to Dr Eric Hyslop and Kimberly John, who allowed us the use of their research on life in streams and rivers.

The big chapter two divides the whole area into six sections, describing features and trails in each. This took much exploration over many months. Jill Byles took it in her stride, involving Hermann Tobisch, myself and others. The book could not have happened without Jill's enthusiastic support and work, nor without the support of Stephen Hodges, who put the script and photos on computer, tidied up the local sketch maps and kept things moving towards publication.

Thanks go to Senator Anthony Johnson for his good advice; to Miss Marilyn Headley, Conservator of Forests, for the use of photographs of trees from the Manual of Dendrology, published by the Forestry Department; to professional photographers Andrew Smith and Jeremy Francis for their help; and to Susan Otouokon and her staff at the Jamaica Conservation and Development Trust office for their continual support and patience.

Finally, thanks to the Environmental Foundation of Jamaica for their continued support of the Natural History Society and our works, starting with their first-ever project, the original Blue Mountain Guide; and to our publishers, Ian Randle Publishers, for being so enthusiastic and patient in taking on this project.

Margaret Hodges
Editor

INTRODUCTION

ROBERT KERR

I love to go a-wandering along the mountain track,
And as I go, I love to sing, my knapsack on my back.
Fal de ri, Fal de ra, my knapsack on my back.
– From the song 'The Happy Wanderer'

A childhood song expresses in its chorus and refrain the kind of joy, happiness and exhilaration one experiences when hiking through the mist and forest to view sunrise from Jamaica's highest point, the Blue Mountain Peak (2,256 m above sea level).

The first publication of the Blue Mountain Guide in 1993 coincided with and gave support to the area's declaration as Jamaica's first terrestrial national park, the Blue and John Crow Mountains National Park.[1] With that declaration came many changes, including the popularisation of the entire area as a tourist destination, along with new measures for its conservation.

The inclusion of the John Crow Mountains within this new protected area opened opportunities for adventure seekers and nature lovers of all sorts. A trek into the rainforest of the Rio Grande Valley offers awesome mountain vistas from every angle, splintered by cascading streams and waterfalls rushing to join the waters of the Rio Grande river. Sunlit trails and

BLUE MOUNTAIN PEAK

pathways give way to shady bamboo avenues with all varieties of clinging and climbing plants; on every side, colourful blooms adorn the banks of the footpaths and tracks. Birdwatchers and photographers are not likely to be disappointed on any excursion into the valley.

The park's designation was accompanied by an increase

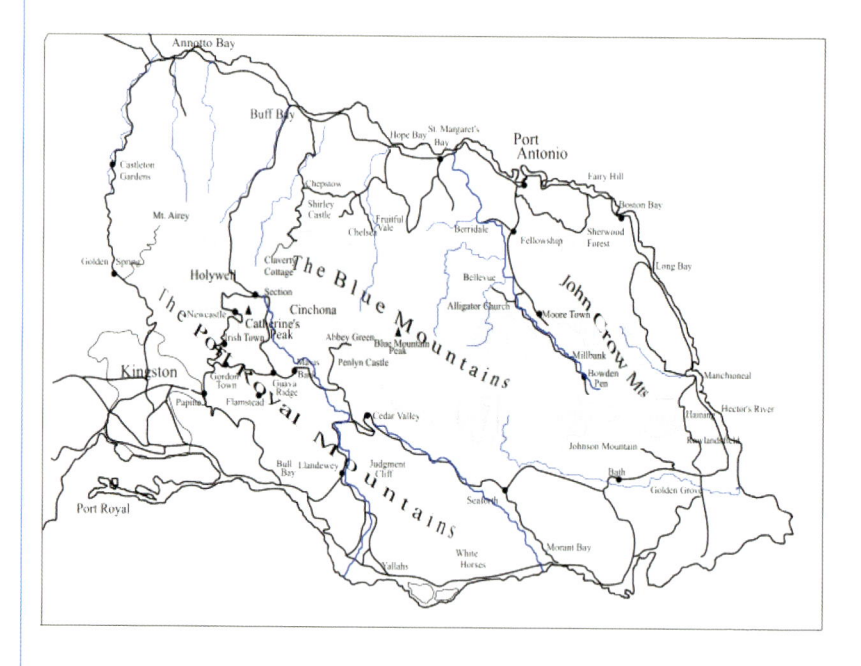

in visitor numbers and subsequently the development of more intense education and outreach programmes in schools and surrounding communities. These measures resulted in a noticeable reduction in the rate of deforestation caused by slash-and-burn farming, a constant threat to the remaining areas of pristine forest. This little-heralded success was in large measure due to the increased environmental awareness and active involvement of several surrounding communities in the conservation of the park and in its tourism services. The Blue Mountain Guide complemented those efforts at awareness building and the enforcement of new regulations to protect the park.

For the past four years, the Jamaica Conservation and Development Trust (JCDT), a national environmental non-governmental organisation (NGO), has managed the area under a delegation agreement with the National Environmental

Protection Agency (NEPA) and a Memorandum of Understanding with the Forestry and Soil Conservation Department (FSCD). Under their stewardship, the infrastructure and services in recreational areas such as Holywell Park and Portland Gap have been greatly improved, adding to visitor enjoyment, comfort and safety. Additionally, research projects conducted within the park have immensely increased the scientific knowledge of the area. Through interpretive displays and signboards, park visitors are informed of the area's rich natural heritage. Holywell Recreational Centre, for example, boasts the Oatley Mountain Trail, a beautifully landscaped and interpreted commercial trail, perhaps the only one of its kind on the island.

Unfortunately, the promise and the tremendous income-generating and recreational potential offered by the approximately 76,000 hectares (196,000 acres) of this park have hardly been tapped. Much of the promised support from government has not been forthcoming, and no system of user fees or other arrangement for the sustained financing of the park was put in place after USAID funding ended. Still outstanding is a permit system for allowing wilderness hikes along a well-managed trail network. Several of the more scenic wilderness trails have been essentially lost – to overgrowth or to landslides or fallen trees in the wake of hurricanes Gilbert and Ivan. Despite the efforts of the JCDT and its partners, the closing years of the last decade witnessed the park's decline and decreasing effectiveness, as government's support remains more rhetorical than tangible.

Given the park's urgent need for revival and support, the publication of this expanded edition of the Blue Mountain Guide, which includes the whole of the national mountain park, is a very timely event. We need to take urgent steps to reverse the degradation of mountain ecosystems. This implies moving the national parks and mountains from the fringes of public consciousness to the top of national and international agendas. Addressing the gaps in public perception of the many ways that mountains directly sustain their well-being is certainly the foremost challenge faced. In this regard, a powerful tool is the transforming close encounter of the natural kind – that first-hand experience of being a 'happy wanderer along the mountain track' – in this instance, the forests of the Blue and John Crow Mountains National Park.

The *Guide to the Blue and John Crow Mountains* tempts and excites the uninitiated, informs and prepares the committed and provides a wonderful memoir for veterans of the experience. From cover to cover, you are taken on a tour in time and space around and through the park. The opening chapters provide an overview, a big picture of the entire area. This is supplemented by descriptions of interesting places, trails, plants and animals. The sections on the human and geological history of the area provide that sense of time travel which weaves everything together into an interesting, informative and enjoyable pocket guide. The Guide to the Blue and John Crow Mountains is an invaluable contribution to Jamaica's conservation literature and movement, and the Natural History Society of Jamaica (NHSJ) should be commended for its perseverance in seeing this project through to completion. Visitors should seek to get a copy of this guidebook before venturing into the national park. It is guaranteed to deepen your appreciation of our mountains and make your trip a more enjoyable experience. We are all indebted to the NHSJ and their sponsors, without whose support this publication would perhaps not have been a reality.

---

1. Established under the USAID/GOJ Protected Area Resource Conservation (PARC) Project (1989–96) as one of two pilot parks, under a programme to establish a system of national parks and protected areas.

TRAVELLING IN THE MOUNTAINS

Margaret Hodges

REACHING THE TRAILS

Buses travel the main roads – from Kingston via Papine to Mavis Bank, or from Kingston via Constant Spring to Stony Hill or Castleton Gardens. A four-wheel-drive vehicle can take you over many of the smaller country roads and forestry tracks to put you nearer to your destination.

The condition of roads and trails changes over time. Flood rains or landslides may block the road rapidly. Bad roads may be improved. Infrequently used trails become overgrown. Local advice may be useful. The environmental non-govermental organization (NGO) responsible for the upkeep of the park is the Jamaica Conservation and Development Trust (JCDT), whose headquarters are at 29 Dumbarton Avenue, Kingston 10. Their postal address is P.O. Box 1225 Kingston 8, and telephone numbers are (876) 920-8278, 920-8279 and 960-2849. They may have information and can also help you with bookings for cabin accommodation at Holywell and at Portland Gap on the Blue Mountain Trail. For further information, please see the appendix. (Note: all telephone numbers to Jamaica begin with the area code 876.)

Another NGO, Valley Hikes, operates from Port Antonio and provides tour guides and information about the areas in the Rio Grande Valley and East Portland area. Contact Vilma Harris, P.O. Box 89, Port Antonio, tel 993-3881. There are also good professional tour operators. More information on all of these can be found in the appendix.

WEATHER

May and October are usually the wettest months, but rain can come in any month. In the hurricane season, June to November, nearby hurricanes can give us much rain and damage. If in doubt, watch the TV weather forecast, check with the Meteorology Office or look for forecasts online.

TIME

Those climbing Blue Mountain Peak often set out from Whitfield Hall, the nearest hostel, at 2 a.m. to reach the Peak by sunrise. Others start at first light to enjoy seeing the changes in vegetation as the path reaches higher levels. In any case, it is best to start early when it is cool and fresh. An early start also ensures that you will see and hear more birds.

In other areas the same principles apply. It is cooler and fresher in the mornings, and more birds are active in the early hours. Birds are also quite active just before dusk, when it is also cooler than at midday.

WHAT TO TAKE AND WEAR

At higher levels it can be cold. Temperatures at Blue Mountain Peak, 2,264 m (7,427 ft), can drop below 4.4°C (40°F) at night, and the mean annual temperature is 13.6°C (56.5°F). The cold, together with mist and rain, can quickly chill the hiker; therefore, carry warm clothing and wind- and rainproof gear. Wear good comfortable shoes or boots and socks. A hat and sunblock cream are useful to keep sun off the face and help prevent skin cancer.

Carry plenty of water, and high-energy food such as raisins, glucose, condensed milk or chocolate. A compass and a map may be very useful. Carry simple first aid such as dressings and a bandage in case of scratches or sprains. Insect repellent is useful in 'tick country' – that is, where cows have been – as well as to keep off mosquitoes, which can be bad in some areas.

If it gets dark before you reach your destination, you will need a torch and spare batteries. A box of matches might be helpful, and a thermos of hot tea, coffee or cocoa would be very welcome.

It is best to travel with a companion or group so that in any real trouble someone can fetch help. The local people are usually very helpful. See the appendix for emergency help.

THE PEAK IN CLOUD

ETIQUETTE

Many laws exist to protect the Park, including the Forestry Act, the Wildlife Protection Act and the Endangered Species Act, but its real protection is the care taken by its users. The ecology is fragile. All those moving through the forest and up the trails

NEAR CINCHONA

are asked to leave as little trace of their passing as possible. This can be done by using the following guidelines, which were written by Paul Steege, an American Peace Corps worker who wrote for the Blue Mountain Guide.

These apply to all regions of the park.

- Carry away with you any garbage you have produced during your visit.

- Burn fires in designated areas only at Portland Gap and the Peak. Use only dead wood, and make sure the fire is out before leaving. Be extra careful about accidental fires that may result from careless use of cigarettes or matches.

- Stay on the trail; it is forbidden to take shortcuts, which eventually result in soil erosion. You can also lose your way going off the trail.

- Be considerate to others by keeping noise to a minimum. Loud radios and loud voices are not appreciated by everyone.

- Do not deface tree trunks, rocks, boulders and signs: do not scratch, mark, paint or spray names or messages on them. Do not damage any plants.

- Do not deface the Forestry structures at Portland Gap or at the Peak.

- Do not disturb the wildlife for example, nesting birds.

- Do not collect plants. Your fellow hiker would like to enjoy them too; and high-elevation plants do not thrive elsewhere.

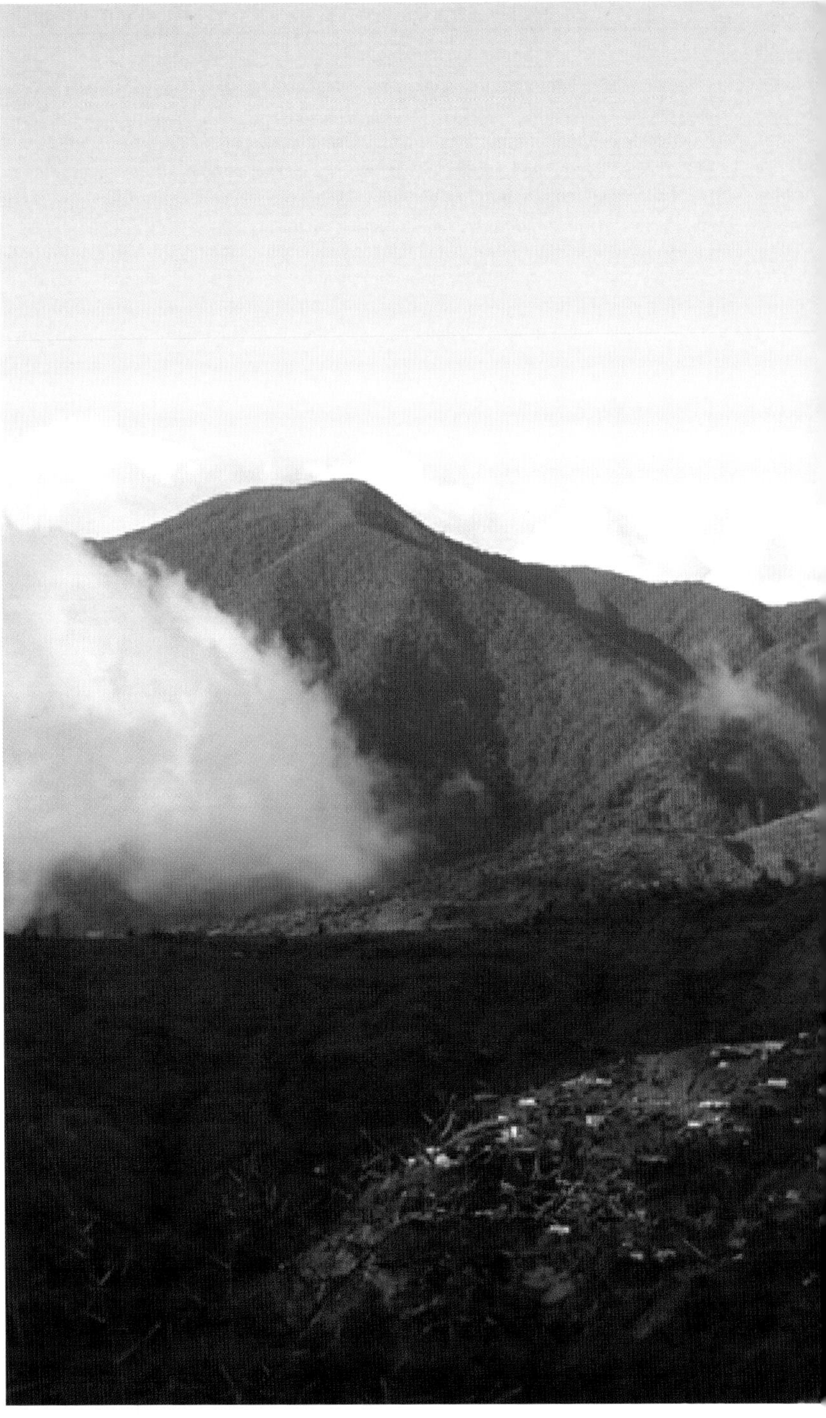

Travelling in the Mountains

THE MAIN RIDGE

THE PARK AND ITS SURROUNDINGS

Jill Byles and Margaret Hodges

This chapter describes the Park and the approaches to it and interesting places to see near the Park and within its boundaries. It is arranged by section, starting with the most westerly.

Looking at the map, you will see that the most westerly section reaches almost to the Junction road, the road that runs from Constant Spring in Kingston to the north coast near Annotto Bay.

The Park spreads south and eastward to Newcastle and Section, where another road from Kingston runs from Papine through Newcastle and Section and turns north to Buff Bay. This is the only road that actually passes right through the Park.

MOUNTAIN STREAM

THE WESTERN SECTION FROM THE JUNCTION ROAD

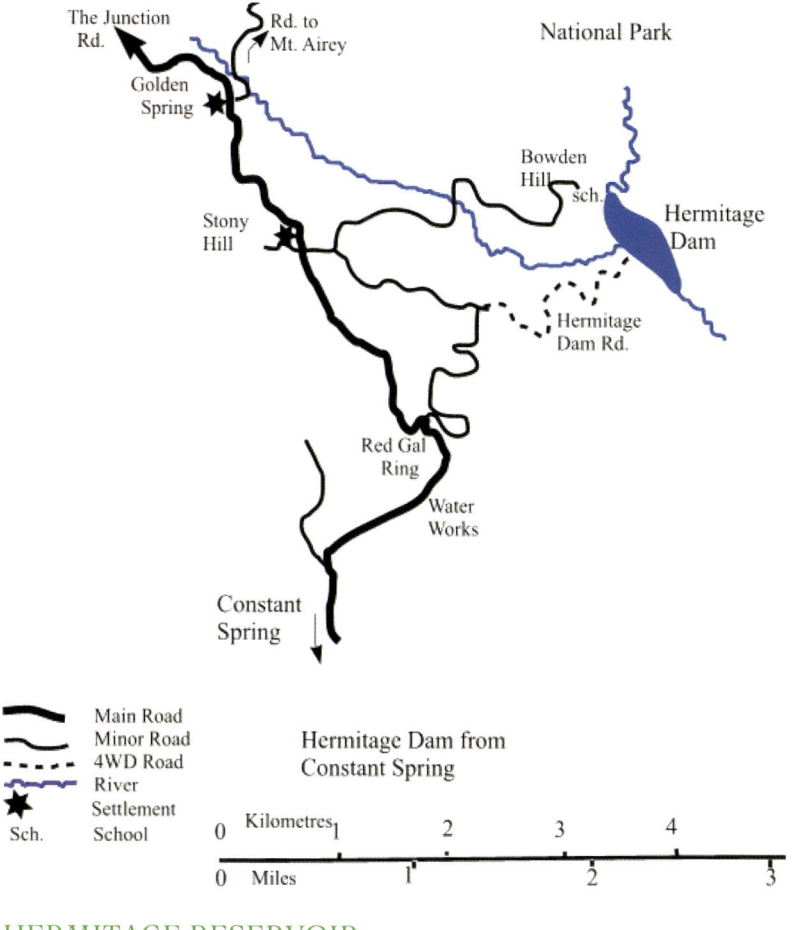

Hermitage Dam from Constant Spring

HERMITAGE RESERVOIR

Soon after leaving Constant Spring there is a large hairpin bend with a gas station on the right. By the gas station, a road leads upward and joins the road from the crossroads at the top of Stony Hill to branch right along the Hermitage Dam road. This large reservoir borders the national park. It is a lovely lake bordered by forest, a good place to see water birds and find water-loving plants. It is maintained by the National Water Commission (NWC), but visitors are allowed so long as they do not contaminate the area or disturb the tranquillity. Large parties are advised to contact the Water Resources Authority for permission to visit; tel 876-927-0077 or 876-702-3952.

HERMITAGE SPILLWAY

The Park and its Surroundings

HERMITAGE DAM LOOKING NORTH

© TREVOR YEE

Guide to the Blue and John Crow Mountains

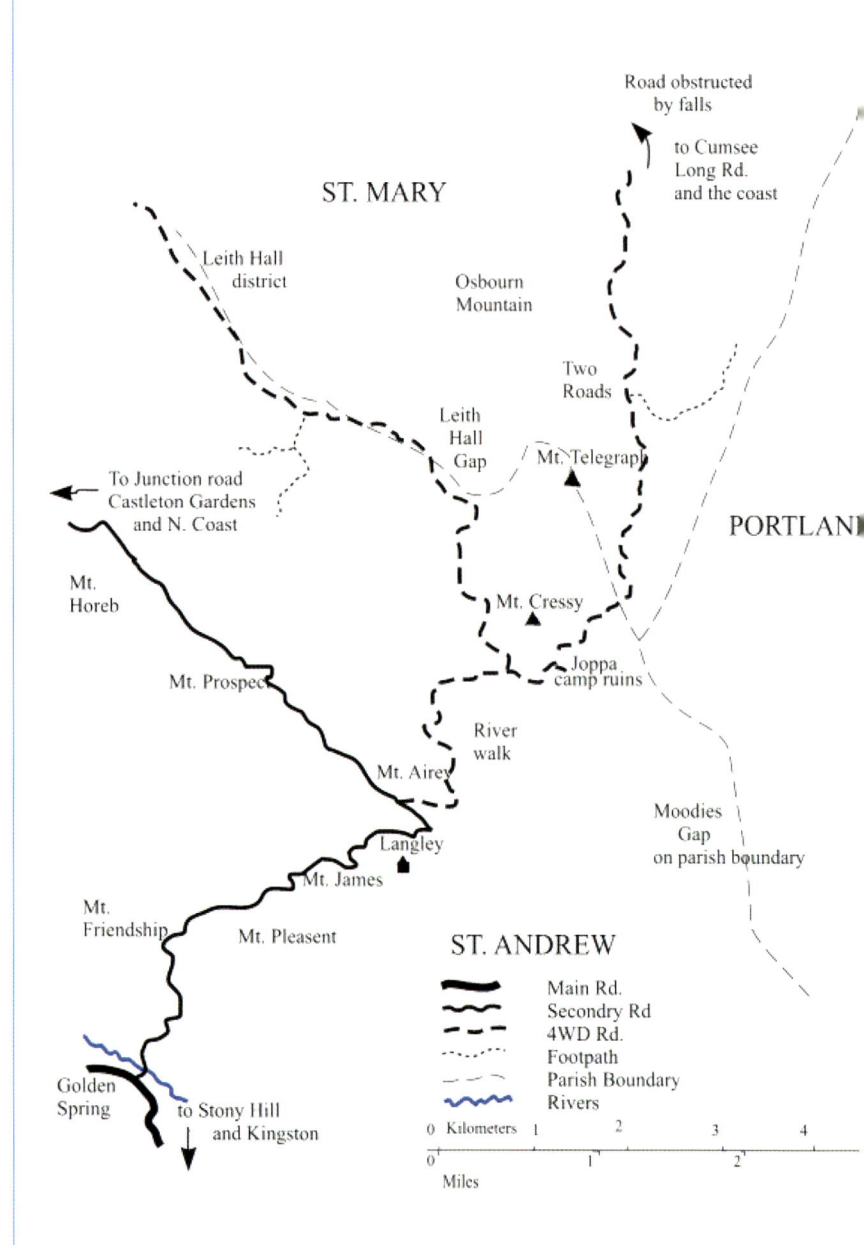

The Park and its Surroundings

LANGLEY

LANGLEY

Beyond Stony Hill lies Golden Spring. As you reach the foot of the hill, there is a road on the right that crosses the river and leads uphill. It goes through a number of small communities and rejoins the Junction road a little before Castleton Gardens, and runs very close to the park borders. After passing Mount Pleasant and Mount James, there is a property on the right, Langley House – the property of the National Water Commission – which can be visited. It was at one time a coffee property, and the remains of the old mill and the barbecues are still there, along with many magnificent old trees and plants. The river runs through on its way to Hermitage, and if you can get permission and a guide you can track down past waterfalls to the dam.

MOUNT AIRY

This is close to Langley. Here you can turn sharp right onto a rather rough forestry road into the national park. The main road leads to a forestry nursery, but beyond it there are disused tracks that offer wonderful views of the hilly land, some open and some wooded, and glimpses of the north coast. Some of these are briefly described.

MOUNTAIN IMMORTELLE

13

RIVER WALK

Within sight of the forestry nursery gates there is a road branching downhill to the left. This leads to a fording which runs through a small stream on its way down to the Wagwater River. This is a beautiful stream, worth stopping and exploring, and a good place for a picnic. To the left, a path with moisture-loving plants on the embankment runs between a large pipe and a stream to a water catchment among tall trees, not far away. A small footbridge to the right crosses another stream, and the path leads through a wooded area and along the left bank of the main stream. The tall trees are mostly blue mahoe, *Hibiscus elatus*, as this was a forestry plantation, but there are others such as the rose apple, and native trees. There are many epiphytes, bromeliads and ferns. The canopy is much enjoyed by birds, especially the flycatchers and woodpeckers, some of which can usually be heard and seen.

Further upstream there are fewer tall trees and more shrubs. There are many small waterfalls, and a bigger one with a pool below. Here, water is collected into the big iron pipe which runs by or under the path to form part of Kingston's water supply.

BEYOND THE FORDING

The road is bad but quite navigable in a four-wheel-drive (4WD) vehicle. Coffee farmers grow their crop on the steep downhill slopes, and on the upper side forestry trees, such as pines and blue mahoe, mingle with bamboos, tree ferns, cedar and broadleaf and the

BLUE MAHOE FLOWER © TREVOR YEE

IRON RIVER MT AIREY © H. TOBISCH

JAMAICAN WOODPECKER © H. VAUGHN

© H. TOBISCH

Guide to the Blue and John Crow Mountains

The Park and its Surroundings

many introduced trees that have spread widely, mangoes and rose apples among them.

Birds such as the Orangequit, Stripe-headed Tanager, White-winged Dove and Zenaida Dove are sometimes seen in the area, and the sound of the Solitaire can often be heard in the distance. About 0.8 km (0.5 mi) further on, the road forks. The road to the right, going east, leads past the ruins of Joppa Boys' Camp and then turns northeast and north to a point where you can look to the sea, and east over the valley to villages and more hills. The other road leads northwest, deep into the forest. Both roads are about 8 km (5 mi) long.

MT. TELEGRAPH

THE ROAD TO THE RIGHT

This leads past the ruins of Joppa Boys' Camp, which was established in the 1970s, and winds uphill to the northeast, where there is an open plateau with views of hills and valleys and the sea to the north. There is an old road near here, running downhill, which turns left and leads up another, very different hill. The road runs along a contour until it is blocked by a fall. Walkers can easily pass this and enjoy the exhilarating moorland-like atmosphere, with views for miles to the north and west. There are few trees but a variety of shrubs, herbs and mosses in the shale-like soil. These include colourful Gesnaria species, ground orchids, club mosses and Selaginella, and the shrub called 'hot lips', *Cephaelis elata*.

Returning to the forestry road and continuing north, the road passes through forest and then runs along the eastern edge.

15

The road used to continue through the villages Cum See and Long Road and link up to the coast, but it is now damaged. Before turning back, however, you can look down on these villages and on the sea between Annotto Bay and Buff Bay, and looking east you can see the double-topped Haycock Hill (1,066 m; 3,500 ft) and many hills behind it.

MOUNT AIREY PINES

COLUMNEA HIRSUTA

GROUND ORCHID (BLETIA SP)

NUN ORCHID

THE ROAD BEARING LEFT

This heads northwest into the forest and has many little roads leading off to coffee plantations. You pass big hills on the right-hand side, some thickly covered with pines. There are some beautiful plants by the roadside: the Jamaican rose, *Blakea trinerva*, with its bright leaves and pink blossoms, and the white-flowered 'English' wild rose, scrambling over other shrubs. Another plant, Tibochina, is similar to the Jamaican rose but has clusters of purple flowers and narrower leaves; it is cultivated in the Botanic Gardens at Castleton. Originally from Polynesia, it has spread and become naturalised in the area.

BLAKEA TRINERVA

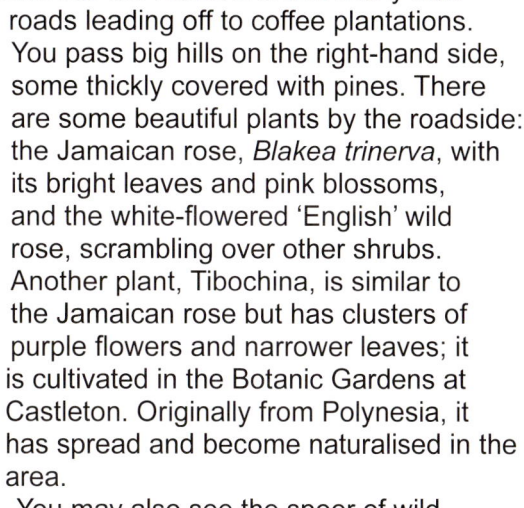

TIBOCHINA

You may also see the spoor of wild pigs that live in the forest. These are the descendants of pigs brought to Jamaica and released by the Spanish in the fifteenth century. They have small tusks and are fierce and fast-moving if disturbed, especially when they have young. They are hunted locally by the young men. It is wise not to stray too far from the road, nor get caught in the area at night.

CASTLETON BOTANIC GARDENS

This most beautiful garden lies about midway along the Junction road between Kingston and the north coast. The road passes through it, dividing it into an upper part that contains the palmetum, fernery, arboretum and formal garden arrangements, and the lower, more informal part, which runs down to and includes the Wagwater River. This part also contains some amazing trees and plants.

The garden has unfortunately suffered much neglect as well as the ravages of floods and hurricanes. It was established in 1862 by the official botanist, Nathaniel Wilson. Great interest was shown by Dr Hooker from Kew Gardens, London, who supplied many specimens and practical help.

Here the Bombay mango, the navel orange and the tangerine were introduced and cultivated, as were many

Guide to the Blue and John Crow Mountains

The Park and its Surroundings

CASTLETON GARDENS

© TREVOR YEE

CYCAD WITH FRUITING BODY

fabulous flowering and useful plants. One was the Pride of Burma (Amherstia nobilis), which flowers in May. Others were the Spathodea, or African tulip, and the poinciana, or flamboyant, now spread throughout the island. Many palms and ferns were introduced, as were the little-known Cycads, which look rather like short, bushy palms but are in fact an ancient group of plants that have survived from the Cretaceous period, over 70 million years ago. There are colourful shrubs, including azaleas, and a flourishing jade vine.

Below the road there are clumps of screw pine or pandanas, a cannonball tree, teak, mahogany, clumps of bamboo and many other interesting plants.

It is a good place to spend a day picnicking by the river, but be prepared for rain. Vendors sell food, drinks and craft items in the parking area.

RECREATIONAL FACILITIES

TAPIOCA VILLAGE RETREAT

Travelling towards the coast from Castleton, the road passes through Devon

WAG WATER RIVER

Guide to the Blue and John Crow Mountains

Pen, in St. Mary, where there are several roadside restaurants that serve local fast food. At a deep corner on the right is Tapioca Village Retreat. It has bread and breakfast (B&B) cabin accommodation and a campsite and offers other meals and guided hikes into the surrounding hills. Tel 876-922-8218 or 876-341-6215, or email tfc-catering@infochan.com.

RIVER'S EDGE

River's Edge is on the Pencar River inland from Annotto Bay, which is east of the Junction road. Take the road inland at the school – the road to Fort George. Cross the new bridge over the Pencar River at Fort George. Keep to your right at the next fork and continue towards the next bridge (Bucket River). After crossing, keep left on the unpaved road until you reach the gate to River's Edge on the left. The last mile is a little bumpy but manageable by cars. Reservations can be made by calling Mrs Chuck at 876-944-2673.

The water is cool and crystal-clear, ideal for bathing. There are picnic shelters, a dormitory, camping and a pleasant walk beside the river that eventually climbs to Monkey Point, which can be seen towering above the valley and overlooking the coast. There used to be roads to settlements further into the hills, but some have been abandoned and may be overgrown. One of these reached Cum See on the way to Mt Airy (see 'Beyond the fording' in this section). Enquire at River's Edge for a guide.

TRANSPORT

Buses and minibuses leave frequently from Constant Spring, Kingston, and from Port Antonio via Annotto Bay to Kingston via the Junction road.

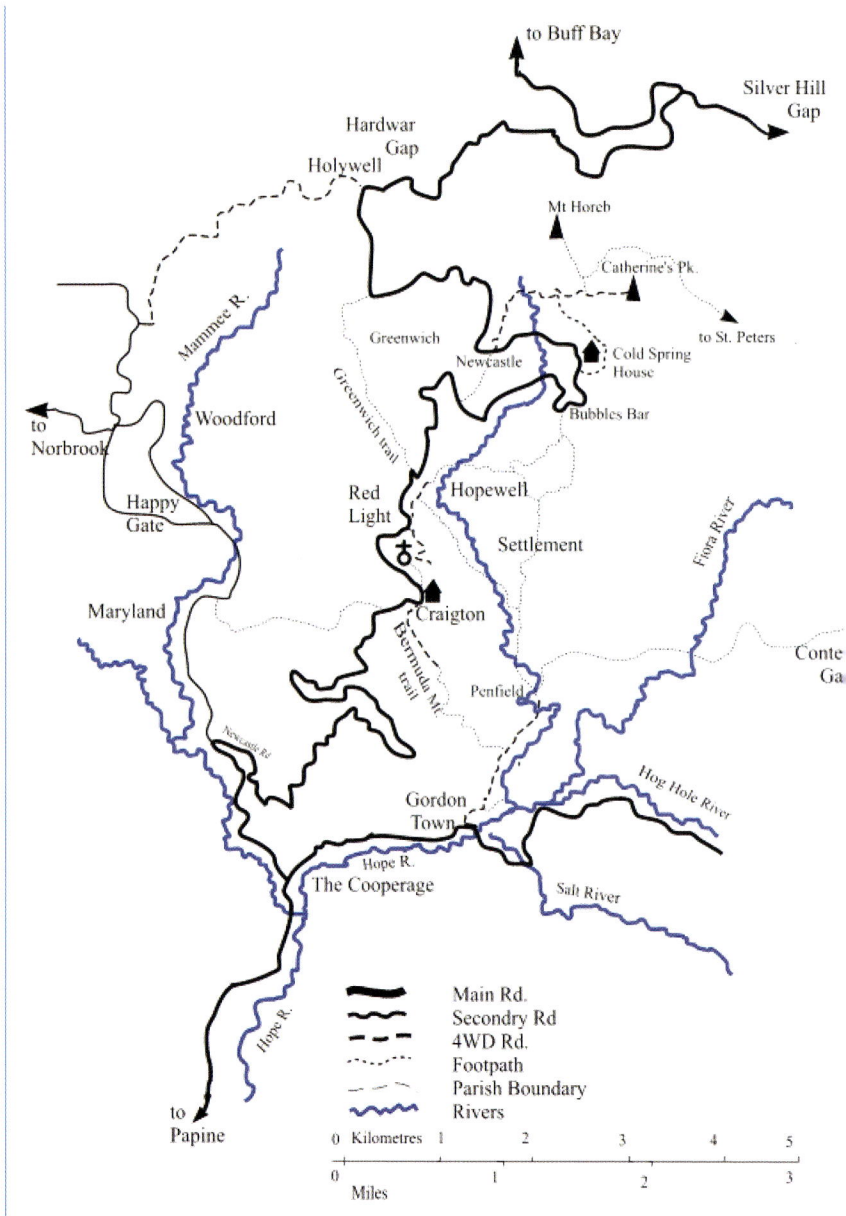

Trails off the Newcastle Rd.
and connecting with Gordon Town

Guide to the Blue and John Crow Mountains

APPROACHES TO THE BLUE MOUNTAINS FROM KINGSTON AND ST. ANDREW

THE SOUTHERN FOOTHILLS FROM PAPINE

The most commonly used approach to the Blue Mountains is by way of the Port Royal Mountains, via Papine, which is at the top of Old Hope Road, a major thoroughfare of the Kingston Metropolitan Area. It is a terminus for buses from all over the Corporate Area. Some of the large white buses go as far as Gordon Town. Minibuses run frequently to Mavis Bank, Irish Town and beyond and through Maryland to Woodford.

For information on Mavis Bank and approaches to the Peak, Gordon Town and trails from the Gordon Town to Guava Ridge road see sections later in this chapter.

Motorists, be warned that there is no petrol station beyond Papine until you reach the coast on the other side of the hills.

MAHOE TREES

SKYLINE DRIVE AND JACK'S HILL

Skyline Drive, 800 m (less than half a mile) on the left after leaving Papine, is a steep climb to a scenic route with a panoramic view of the city spread out below. The road leads through Jack's Hill Village, which has an active environmentally concerned Citizens' Association, and back down to the city via Barbican Square. Several trails along the road lead into the valley of the Mammee River, to Maryland, Woodford and Peter's Rock,

EBONY IN FLOWER

23

and join routes that go further into the hills. They are all likely to be overgrown. The best-known guide to the area is Tony Mitchell, who lives beside the shop in Jack's Hill (tel 876-702-0143).

PAPINE TO NEWCASTLE

Follow the road from Papine along the Hope River Gorge, over the bridge at Blue Mountain Inn, and immediately turn left at The Cooperage. The name refers to the Irish coopers who constructed the wooden barrels in which Blue Mountain coffee beans were shipped in the nineteenth century. This road leads to Newcastle and Holywell.

STREAM IN BANK

OLD MAN'S BEARD

MARYLAND

The next left turn, 3 km (2 mi) further on, runs beside the Mammee River to Maryland, Woodford and Cambridge, from where it is possible to return to the city via the suburb of Norbrook. A road to the left climbs higher, to Happy Gate and Peter's Rock, which has magnificent views. The rough road to the right goes though coffee farms to the bottom of Holywell Nature Reserve and is better for hiking than driving. The reserve is 3.5 km (2.25 mi) away, with good views along the way but not much shade. Minibuses run from Papine to Woodford.

Dustry Road, a sharp, steep turn off the Maryland road, reaches the Newcastle road at the bottom of Irish Town. Just before it makes a sharp right, there is an entrance to a property. This is Dry Hill Road, which leads to Strawberry Hill resort at the top of Irish Town. Also from Maryland, by the bridge festooned

NEWCASTLE

with satellite dishes, is the beginning of the Mount Edward trail to Redlight, just beyond Irish Town.

IRISH TOWN AND REDLIGHT

Irish Town is a pleasant residential area stretching along the main road for some distance. Some of the older residences have Irish place names, as this was where the Irish coopers who made the coffee barrels lived. Crystal Edge is a restaurant and bar squeezed between a precipice on one side and the road on the other. It serves tasty, filling Jamaican dishes at reasonable prices.

For gracious surroundings and dining, try Strawberry Hill,

STRAWBERRY HILL

25

hill, where charming cottages nestle against the hillside among verdant vegetation (tel 876-944-8400 or 876-944-8408; for details see appendix). Just along the main road on the right, at Craighton, is the Japanese-owned Ueshima coffee farm and Great House. Tours can be arranged (tel 876-944-8224). Beside it is Bermuda Mount Road, which becomes a trail down to the right just before the road ends. Above is the Bermuda Mount property. The trail, which takes less than an hour to walk, enters Gordon Town just above the post office, beside a gatepost labelled 'Rawcliffe'. It passes through stands of bamboo and smallholdings and offers some good views.

VIEW FROM STRAWBERRY HILL

It combines well with the old path linking Gordon Town and Redlight, thought to have been the 'red-light district' for the military at Newcastle. A short distance away is a steep footpath

CRAIGTON CHURCH

BUBBLES BAR

MEXICAN DAISIES

to Craighton church, which has a splendid view. The driving road to the church, also steep, is at Redlight. Beside it is the old rough road down to Gordon Town, beside the Hope River. A left branch, through Hopewell, passes old Middleton coffee barbecues. It crosses a bridge and becomes a rocky track before reaching the very steep asphalt road that leads uphill through Middleton to Bubbles Bar and Grocery, on the main road, not far below Newcastle. A track leading off the asphalt road just below a very large retaining wall goes to Settlement, at which point the asphalt road meets it again. Along this road is a small bar run by a woman called Del, who welcomes visitors. This is a productive farming community in which the EU and the Rural Agricultural Development Authority (RADA) have special interests.

The road continues as a wooded trail down to the right, along the side of the Hope River valley, until it meets the trail from Redlight to Gordon Town, already mentioned, which also runs along the Hope River valley but at a lower level. A combination of any of these roads and trails through Middleton, Settlement, Redlight and Hopewell makes a very pleasant walk lasting two or three hours.

RUELLA

Between Redlight and Newcastle on the main road are two trails off to the left. The first, the Copper Gully or Greenwich trail, is on a sharp right bend beside a bridge over a stream surrounded by ginger lilies. It is a shortcut, climbing through Caribbean pine trees and coffee, to attractive residences on Greenwich Drive, which is between Newcastle and Holywell Nature Reserve. The entrance to the other trail, a steep, rugged cattle track, is at a gate marked 'Dell'. This trail reaches Newcastle, passing beside the military cemetery. Also between Redlight and Newcastle, accommodation and meals – and a remarkable view – are available at Mount Edge, a house that clings to the hillside just below the road (tel 876-944-8392; US$30 for B&B, double). Tours can also be arranged.

THE HERITAGE GARDENS OF COLD SPRING

Cold Spring (now known as Heritage Gardens), once a coffee estate, can be seen to the right as one approaches Newcastle. It is almost opposite the Catherine's Peak Spring Water bottling plant. The house, surrounded by bright flowers, stands above the old coffee barbecues. It was once owned by

BRILLANTASIA OWARIENSIS

HERITAGE GARDENS

Guide to the Blue and John Crow Mountains

The Park and its Surroundings

Matthew Wallen, an Irish naval officer and botanist, who came to Jamaica in 1747. He introduced plants to Jamaica including bamboo, watercress and nasturtiums, and his gardens grew varieties of temperate-climate plants. There are still some to be seen, along with many different trees that attract birds. The present owner makes the property available for functions, and a cottage can be rented. There is an interpretive centre in the main house. Call 876-960-0794 or 876-929-9481.

Tree Tops, where a comfortable two-bedroom home can be rented, is in the same area, located on the spring that is the source of Catherine's Peak Spring Water. The rate per night is US$80. For details, email bluejamaica@kasnet.com.

NEW CASTLE AND ITS SURROUNDINGS

The road runs through the centre of the parade ground of the military camp at Newcastle, from which there is a fine view of Kingston 1,200 m (4,000 ft) below. Flanked by cannons, the wall opposite bears the insignia of the regiments that have been stationed here. Newcastle's red-roofed buildings climbing the hill are a prominent landmark from the city and other locations.

(See chapter 2, 'The Historical Background', for the history of Newcastle).

Just below Heritage Gardens is a rough track, passing behind the former estate and other attractive homes on the way to Newcastle. After a while it becomes a foot trail leading to a well-maintained road. It goes through the military camp to the parade ground. Along the road is a signposted intersection. The paved right fork, which runs very steeply through montane forest, is the road to Catherine's Peak, which reaches an altitude of 1,600 m (5,060 ft). The peak takes its name from the first woman said to have climbed it, in 1760, the sister of the historian Edward Long and the wife of Jamaica's lieutenant governor from 1756 to

BELOW NEWCASTLE

BLUE MOUNTAIN BEGONIA

1759, Henry Moore. (This precedes the claim that it was named for the owner of a coffee plantation there, Catherine de La Harpe, who fled with others following the revolution in St Dominique, now Haiti, in the 1790s.) When the mist clears, there are excellent views in all directions – though, not surprisingly, marred by numerous masts and satellite dishes. The lower left fork, where moisture encourages thick vegetation at the start, leads to an attractively maintained private property, Clifton Mount, next to which is a footpath to St. Peters on the road between Section and Guava Ridge. There is a plant nursery, and coffee is grown on the surrounding slopes.

CARIBBEAN PINES

The road to Catherine's Peak originates in the parade ground at Newcastle and is controlled by the military authority. Requests to drive to the peak may not always be granted.

Some of the trails have been overgrown with bush, but there are plans to restore some in the future. A new fern trail has been opened near the left turnoff on the Catherine's Peak road to Clifton Mount, near the top.

HARDWAR GAP AND HOLYWELL NATURE RESERVE

Between Newcastle and Hardwar Gap are paved roads to the left that lead to some attractive homes at Greenwich and also to the Copper Gully trail back down to the Newcastle road. Before cars, the trail would have been a major route to Hardwar

The Park and its Surroundings

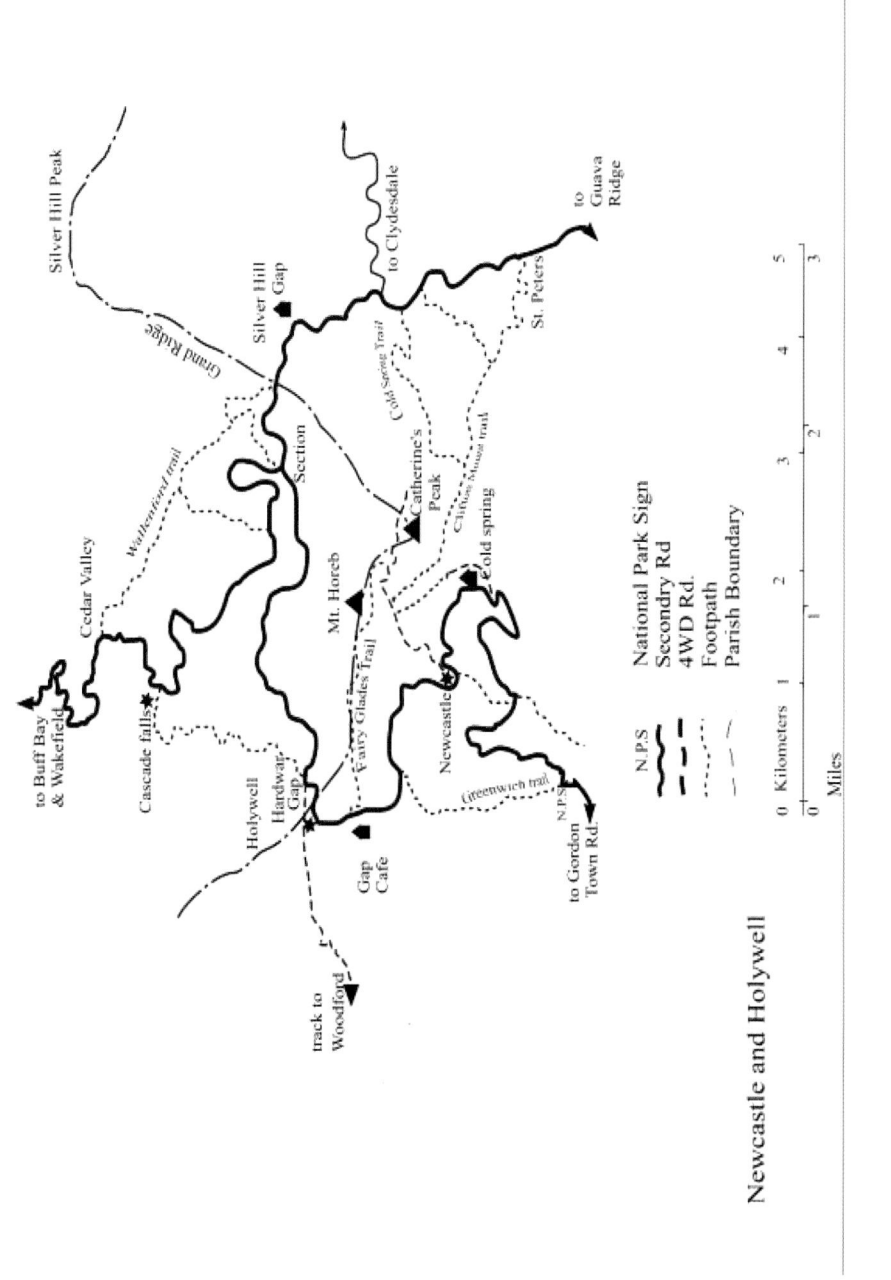

Newcastle and Holywell

CATHERINE'S PEAK FROM CLIFTON MOUNT ROAD

The Park and its Surroundings

YELLOW GINGER LILY

GINGER LILY SEED PODS

LICHEN

LYCOPODIUM

Gap and Portland.

The parishes of St. Andrew and Portland meet at Hardwar Gap. This may have been named for the auditor general in 1782, though another story has it that a British Army officer previously stationed in India named it after a famous beauty spot in the Himalayas.

Near the park entrance is the Gap Café and Gift Shop, which also provides accommodation (B&B US$60; tel 876-923-7078 or 876-997-3032; see appendix for details).

There is a noticeable change in vegetation and climate at Hardwar Gap, where on most days mist descends on one of Jamaica's few remaining montane forest areas. Ginger lilies grow thickly on the roadside. Holywell Nature Reserve, a recreational area, is on the left. The entrance fee is J$100, children $50. Since 1993 it has been part of the Blue and John Crow Mountains National Park. The reserve offers a view of Kingston, picnic spots, tents and tent spaces, and cabins that can be rented from the JCDT (see appendix for details). There are several trails through the forest, and guides are available. Near the entrance there is an interpretive centre. The Oatley trail is of particular interest. It passes through tall tree ferns and trees bearing epiphytes, such as wild pines, orchids,

HOLYWELL TRAIL

HOLYWELL ENTRANCE

Guide to the Blue and John Crow Mountains

The Park and its Surroundings

GAZEBO

HOLYWELL CABINS

37

HOT LIPS

BROMELIAD

TREE FERNS

ferns, lichens and fungi, through fern brakes and mossy sections. Guides explain and watch for birds and other wildlife. There is a charge for use of this trail. Many of the birds described in chapter 8 can be seen or heard early in the morning or in the evening. It is rare not to hear the distinctive sounds of Solitaires calling to each other – a high, sustained whistle followed by a lower note and sometimes a trill.

Behind the parking area is the Waterfall trail, with several farm roads leading off it. Avoid these and bear right, across a level area planted in eucalyptus trees. It is then possible to follow a narrow, steep downhill track, which eventually reaches the road to Buff Bay beside a scenic waterfall. The trail is crossed by another path. Left leads out, further down the Buff Bay valley, so turn right for the waterfall, and keep to the right on reaching some dwellings.

The Park and its Surroundings

BUFF BAY VALLEY

YACCA

COFFEE IN BUFF BAY VALLEY

HAYCOCK HILL

Then turn left, down onto a wider track.

Just past the Holywell entrance, now in Portland, there is a steep track leading down to the Olde Tavern Coffee Estate, where the Twymans grow organic coffee. It was once a staging post for travellers crossing from one side of the island to the other, and it can still be used to reach the Buff Bay road on foot. A tour can be arranged (see appendix), and the coffee is for sale. There is another entrance on the main road.

Along the road there are some weekend cottages with brilliant exotic gardens; some of them are available for rental. Trees, houses and banks of hydrangeas, azaleas, fuchsias,

39

nasturtiums and impatiens appear through the mist in ghostly fashion or glow in dappled light. This area is recommended to the birdwatcher, particularly in the early morning and in the evening. The flora is an interesting mix. Some meadow plants came in with fodder for the army's horses, which was shipped from Europe from 1841 for some years. Wild strawberries and violets can be found on the grassy banks. On the left, beside a wooden shop, is the start of the Green Hills trail, which drops steeply to the Buff Bay road beside Cascade school.

At Section the scenic road continues left down to Buff Bay (see 'The Northern Section') or turns sharp right to Silver Hill Gap, St. Peters, with a route to Clydesdale, Cinchona, Content Gap and downhill to the Guava Ridge intersection.

COFFEE FLOWER

COFFEE BERRIES

SECTION TO ST. PETERS

SECTION COFFEE TOUR

Guide to the Blue and John Crow Mountains

The Park and its Surroundings

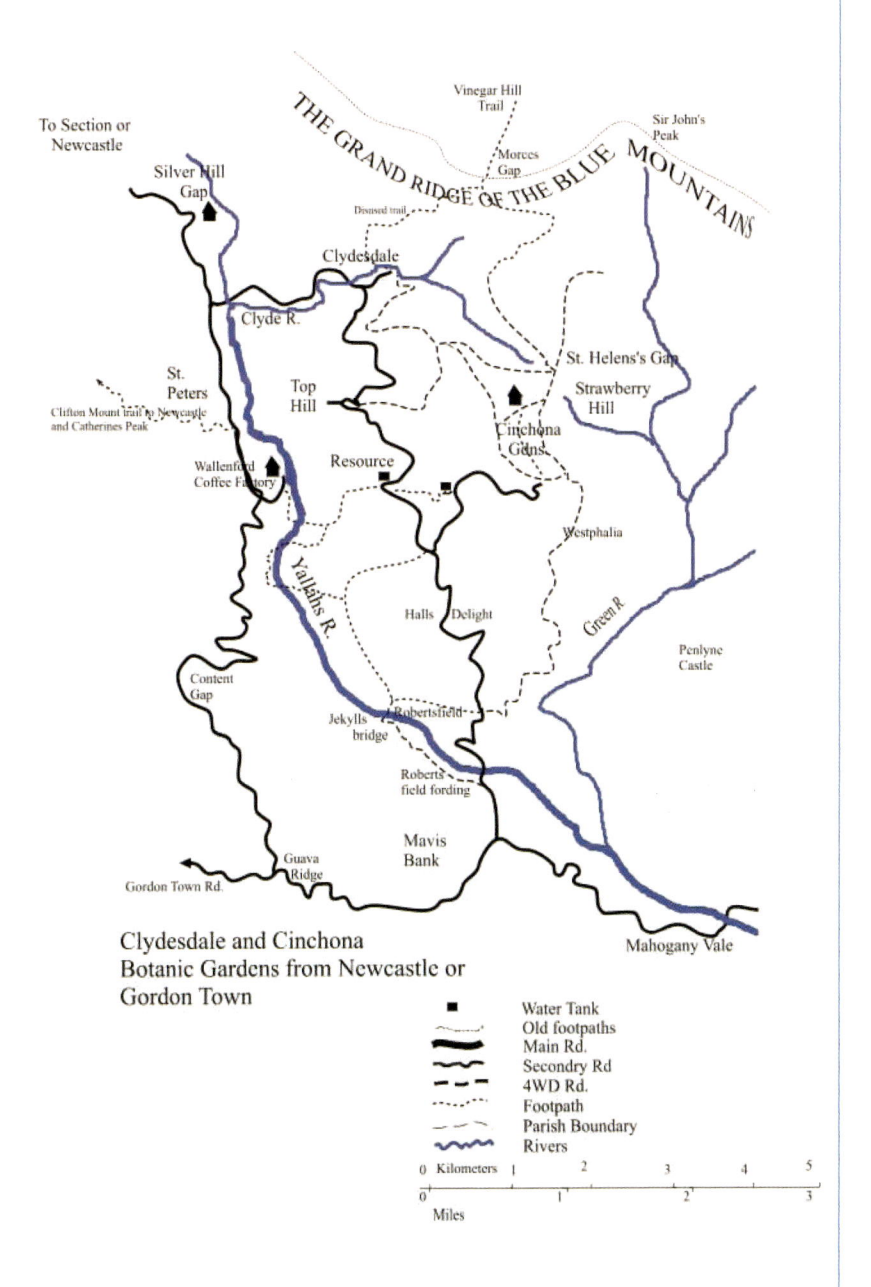

Clydesdale and Cinchona Botanic Gardens from Newcastle or Gordon Town

SILVER HILL GAP

Silver Hill Gap, between Section and St. Peters, used to be a major intersection. A very steep road, through Forestry Department land to the right, went to Newcastle via St. Catherine's Peak. Now, after a mile uphill between coffee trees, it disappears into the surrounding bracken, but there are some good views of the mountains. Early in the year the road is dotted with tiny mauve violets with arrow-shaped leaves.

To the north at Silver Hill Gap is a rough road, the Wallenford trail – named for Matthew – which runs to Cedar Valley, where it joins the main driving road from Section to Buff Bay.

There is an old house with an azalea garden at Candlelight, Silver Hill Gap, and adjacent to it, facing the mountains, is Starlight Chalet & Health Spa, a more modern building with comfortable accommodation. At night there are no lights to spoil the starry sky. There are double and single rooms and an extra charge for meals. Pauline is an efficient chef who can produce a fresh cooked meal in very little time. Call 876-906-3075 or 876-969-3116.

On the right, approaching St. Peters, is the trail to Clifton Mount. Look for the sign on the roadside.

TODY

FLOWERING CHEESEBERRY

APPROACHES TO CLYDESDALE AND CINCHONA BOTANIC GARDENS

There are several routes to Cinchona. All of them are challenging.

A turn-off, leading to a former forestry nursery at Clydesdale and a track to Cinchona Botanic Gardens, is on the left at St. Peters. Do not attempt to take a low vehicle on this two-mile stretch of road. At Clydesdale, the remains of a coffee pulpery include some old buildings, barbecues and the mill wheel. The

The Park and its Surroundings

property later became a forestry nursery, where Caribbean pine seedlings were grown. It was opened to the public, offering a lovely spot for camping and the upper part of the forester's house for rental.

Since 1988, when hurricane Gilbert flattened thousands of pines, the nursery has been left to decay, but campers still make use of the site, and it is still beautiful with its rivers and pools, and trails leading towards Morces Gap (not maintained) and to Cinchona. Below the buildings is a river pool deep enough for a very refreshing swim. Routes to Cinchona are across the stream behind the mill. The shorter route to the left is described

RED SALVIA

CLYDESDALE FORESTRY HOUSE

43

WILD STRAWBERRIES

CUPRESSUS

under 'Cinchona Botanic Gardens' (see p. 46).

A 4WD vehicle can sometimes reach the Gardens by the road to the right from Clydesdale. This road eventually reaches the Yallahs River fording at Robertsfield, near Mavis Bank, but there is a road to Cinchona off to the left, opposite the water tank at Resource (or Top Mountain). Further along, at Hall's Delight, there is another turning that will lead up to Cinchona. Good nerves are needed for this journey, although the views are spectacular. These two roads join before entering the bottom of Cinchona Gardens. The junction has a good parking spot.

If you are approaching Cinchona from Mavis Bank via the Yallahs River fording at Robertsfield, the left road goes to Hall's Delight and the right to Westphalia, from which a foot path joins the road to the bottom of the gardens. Behind the Westphalia school is a trail down to the Green River, which then climbs to Penlyne Castle. The route is not easy, as it is intersected by many cattle and farm tracks.

These roads are inaccessible if the Yallahs River is high. However, there is a good hiking trail, which starts as a rough road beside the Wallenford coffee factory near St. Peters. It is accessible by vehicle as far as a footbridge over the Yallahs River. On

COFFEE BUILDINGS

Guide to the Blue and John Crow Mountains

The Park and its Surroundings

ROSEAPPLE FLOWER

YALLAS AT WALLENFORD

the other side, take the uphill trail (trails off to the right lead back to the river). It climbs through a settlement to Resource and nearby Top Mountain, cutting out many miles of road. Then take one of the previously described roads to Cinchona.

The river trail follows the Yallahs River from the Wallenford coffee factory down to Robertsfield, near Mavis Bank. It takes two hours of fairly easy walking, except for having to wade across the river twice. After crossing the first bridge, you will see several trails going off to the left. Always keep right, unless you want to go to Resource or Hall's Delight to pick up a Cinchona trail. At Robertsfield the path crosses the Jeckyll bridge, constructed in the early 1900s. It is a reminder of a garden established nearby by Walter Jeckyll, brother of the British garden designer Gertrude Jeckyll.

NEAR ROBERTSFIELD

Keep left, unless you wish to climb to the Content Gap road at Quashie Gap.

CINCHONA BOTANIC GARDENS

After leaving Clydesdale from behind the mill, the route to the left to Cinchona is best done on foot. It is very steep in places. The hillsides now grow coffee, but tea was cultivated here when Cinchona was founded in 1868. It takes an hour or more to reach the intersection at St. Helen's Gap. To the far left is the Vinegar Hill trail, and branching off it to the right is a trail that leads through coffee plants to Sir John's Peak. Turn up to the right to enter the gardens. As you come into the gardens, you are at the top of the panoramic walk on the east face, with magnificent views of the Grand Ridge of the Blue Mountains and St Thomas beyond. Benches invite you to rest and absorb the view, the fresh air and peace of the mountains.

The cinchona trees gradually died out, but there are still many diverse trees and shrubs from mountainous areas all

BLUE IRIS

CINCHONA

Guide to the Blue and John Crow Mountains

The Park and its Surroundings

over the world that were cultivated years ago. The Rhododendrons and Azaleas, whose vast trunks give away their age, bloom best in the early spring. Many trees, especially the tall ones, were blown down in hurricane Gilbert in 1988. Others remain: the tall cork tree (*Quercus suber*) and the nearby camphor trees (*Cinnamomum camphora*) are in good health. There are many varieties of eucalyptus from Australia and conifers from all over the world, including Jamaica's juniper cedar (*Juniperus barbutensis*) and yacca (*Podocarpus urbanii*). There is an ancient Japanese cedar still standing on the lawn below the governor's house. Many species of lilies bloom, mostly in early summer; the massed Agapanthus are most spectacular. At the top of the gardens is the old governor's house, behind which are striking displays of Cymbidium orchids.

CINCHONA

CINCHONA

AGAPANTHUS

CLYDESDALE EUCALYPTUS

AZALEAS

THE VINEGAR HILL TRAIL

TREE ORCHID
© HAGERMAN AND STEWART

BROMELIADS
© S. HODGES

Several trails once converged on Cinchona, linking the gardens with Sir John's and John Crow peaks and going on to Blue Mountain Peak, but most are now impassable.

The Vinegar Hill trail can be approached from the St Helen's Gap intersection; keep to the left. It is one of the oldest thoroughfares in Jamaica. It once was part of a network of tracks used by horse-drawn vehicles travelling through working estates between the island's south and north coasts.

Now overgrown by forest and rarely used, it goes via Morces Gap, below Sir John's Peak, through a tree-lined glade festooned with orchids, ferns and bromeliads. It once reached the north coast by way of Thompson Gap, Claverty Cottage, Chepstow and Skibo, along the Spanish River and out to Spring Garden. Unless you have made prior arrangements with an experienced guide from the area, turn back as soon as it becomes difficult to make out the trail.

ST. PETERS TO GUAVA RIDGE

To the left of the road between St. Peters and Content Gap is a panoramic view of the mountains, with populated hills in the foreground and Cinchona and Blue Mountain Peak behind. Opposite the large white church of Mount Lebanon, a rough driving road leads through coffee farms to a panoramic view of Kingston and the coast. A footpath from a flight of steps near Content Gap also goes there. From the water tank in the road at Content Gap a trail leads right, down to Gordon Town. This is the Sugarloaf trail, described in the section on Gordon Town (see pp. 69–72) and map 3.

The main road climbs to Quashie Gap and then drops

The Park and its Surroundings

CINCHONA FROM ST. PETER'S ROAD

steeply to Guava Ridge. A rough road to the left at Quashie Gap goes to the residential area of Salt Hill. The road deteriorates into a track, dropping steeply via Penny Hill to Mavis Bank. There are some magnificent views of the coast and the Grand Ridge.

Roads to Gordon Town, Mavis Bank and Flamstead meet at Guava Ridge intersection.

GUAVA RIDGE TO MAVIS BANK

Eastward from Guava Ridge, take the road downhill to Mavis Bank. Hikers can take a shortcut on a parochial road (parochial is the Jamaican and English word used for local roads and bridle paths which should be maintained by the parish — bridle paths were originally used by horsemen

PEPPER HIBISCUS

and pedestrians), which starts on the right beside a bar at the bottom of Guava Ridge and meets the main road again further downhill. At a bridge, the main road divides. To the right, the road fords the Fall River and passes the entrance to Mavis Bank Central Coffee Factory and then continues to Tower Hill and Limetree. The factory is the oldest and largest of Jamaica's working coffee factories. To arrange a tour of the factory, call 876-977-8005.

For further walks in this area, see the Tower Hill and Limetree section.

The factory can be seen below the Mavis Bank road. On the Mavis Bank road, just beyond the factory and opposite the Wesleyan Church, is Forres Park, which offers accommodation in the main house and in wooden cabins. There are kitchens, and catering is also done on the premises. It is a working coffee farm, with many varieties of fruit trees which attract many species of birds. Tel 876-927-8275.

Visitors who wish to climb to the Peak can overnight at Abbey Green at the foot of the trail, by arrangement made at Forres Park.

Mavis Bank is nearby. A parochial road almost opposite Forres Park bypasses Mavis Bank and follows the Fall River to Mount Charles.

LOOKING DOWN ON MAVIS BANK

MAVIS BANK

Minibuses run from Papine to Mavis Bank and back. Mavis Bank is a small town serving the communities on the south slopes of Blue Mountain Peak. Almost everyone heading for the Peak passes through Mavis Bank. From here, 4WD vehicles head for Hagley Gap and Penlyne Castle, on the way to the Peak. The route is via Mt Charles by the Fall River and then to Mahogany Vale, where it meets the Yallahs River. Drivers charge according to the number of passengers. There are

The Park and its Surroundings

several shops, so this is the place to provision. It is also the place to inquire about guides and the condition of the trails. The police station is a good place to start. Let the officers on duty know your plans. If you are driving, ask them about parking in Mavis Bank and the condition of the roads you plan to drive on. Heavy rains may occur anytime between May and December, washing out mountain roads and trails or causing landslides that block them.

CUPRESSUS

Just at the start of Mavis Bank Top Road is a container that has been converted into a restaurant, very popular with the locals. Here, Mr Roy can advise on vehicles and guides to the Peak. In the early evening there are always vehicles going to Hagley Gap and Penlyne. The cost is around J$2,000. The guiding rate, one-way from Penlyne, is

CUPRESSUS

about J$1,500. Be prepared to haggle. To avoid the competing drivers and guides, make prior arrangements through one of the following: JCDT (876-920-8278 or 876-920-8279), Whitfield Hall Hostel and Farm (876-927-0986, 876-995-1766, 876-995-5776) or Wild Flower Lodge, Forres Park (876-927-8275). Also ask them about accommodation, which ranges from very basic to modestly luxurious. Bed and breakfast is available with Ms Joyce Bennett on Mavis Bank Top Road (876-977-8360). She can also advise on a reliable guide if you wish to walk to the Peak from Mavis Bank.

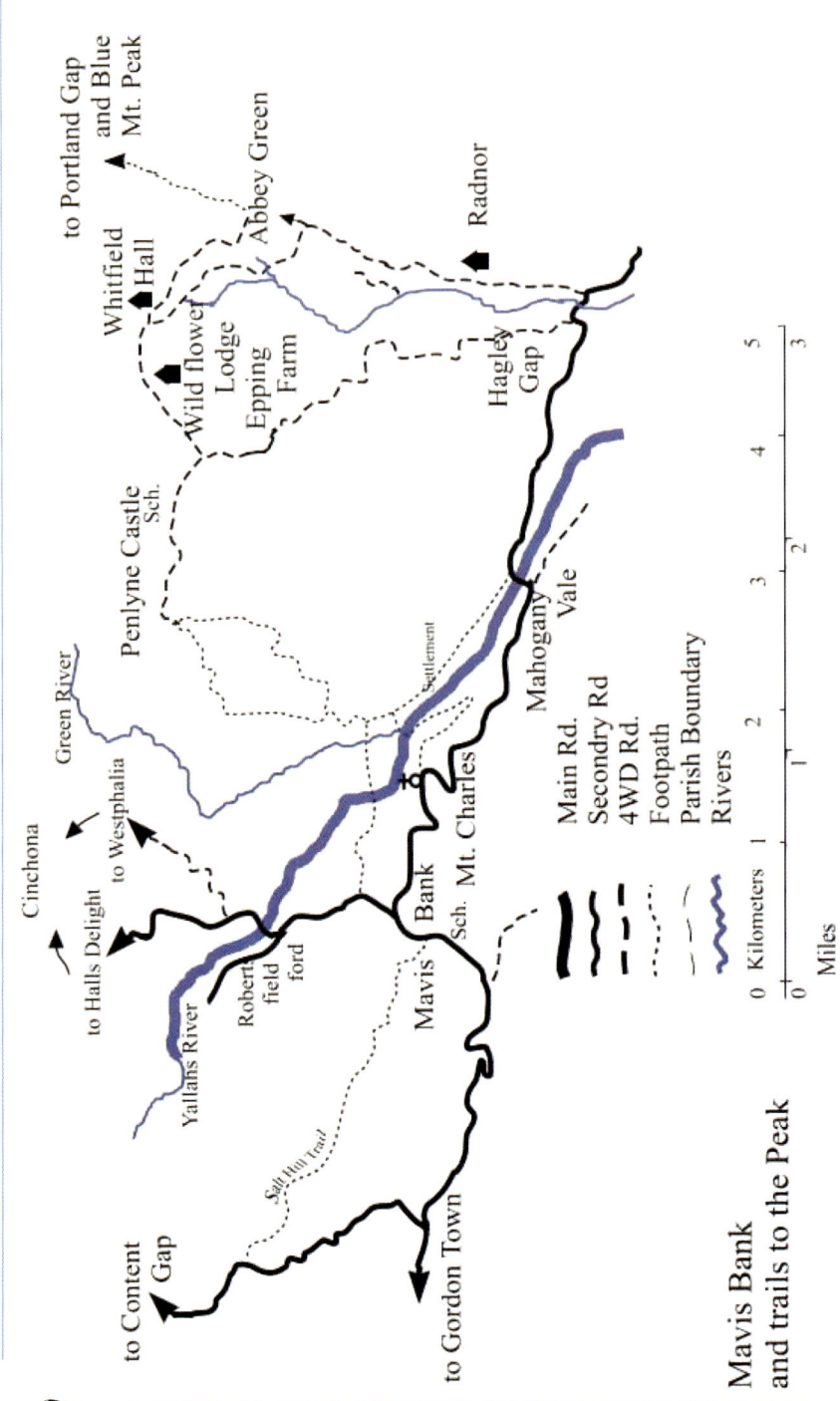

Mavis Bank and trails to the Peak

MAVIS BANK TO PENLYNE CASTLE

MAHOGANY VALE YALLAHS FORDING

PENLYNE CASTLE

MOUNTAIN PRIDE

It takes one and a half to two hours to walk from Mavis Bank to Penlyne Castle on the way to the Peak. Take the turning to Robertsfield, beside the Anglican Church. A short distance on the right, beside some wooden shops, is a narrow right turn. It leads to Yallahs River. Cross it and walk beside the river to where the Green River meets it. Cross the Green River and start the ascent to Penlyne. Where the path forks, go right to reach the school and the driving road from Hagley Gap, or turn left to reach the same road further on, at a standpipe and a house surrounded by coffee trees. Continue along the road past Wildflower Lodge and Whitfield Hall to Abbey Green, where the Blue Mountain Peak trail begins. These three hostels offer accommodation by prior arrangement.

MOUNT CHARLES TO PENLYNE CASTLE

The road through Mavis Bank goes to Mount Charles. Scorpio Inn here has rooms to rent. Tel 942-7912-3. If a lift is available, use this route rather than the one previously mentioned. If it is dry, take the road on the left beside the Kingdom Hall church. It drops steeply to Settlement, where there are a playing field and a small group of houses. Here the Green River meets the Yallahs. Cross the river where footpaths lead up to a track running parallel to the river. Turn left and continue until you meet a steep trail to the right, which leads to Penlyne. If the river is high, the same track can be reached by crossing the bridge at Mahogany Vale and turning left.

REACHING THE BLUE MOUNTAIN PEAK TRAIL BY ROAD

RADNOR ROAD

The trail to Blue Mountain Peak begins at Abbey Green; it can be reached in several ways. A 4WD vehicle can be driven from Mavis Bank down to the Yallahs River at Mahogany Vale, where you can cross the river and drive to Hagley Gap. From here a very steep road leads to Epping Farm. Bearing right, you pass Wildflower Lodge and Whitfield Hall and reach Abbey Green, above which the trail begins.

Another route from Hagley Gap is to turn downhill to the Negro River, where there is a fording and pedestrian bridge. In wet weather the fording is often impassable. A rough track then leads left through the former coffee estate of Radnor. It is privately owned and the road privately maintained with wire

TREE FERN

gates across it at two places, which can be lifted aside but must be replaced. The track emerges near Whitfield Hall. Turn right for Abbey Green.

THE PEAK TRAIL

The trail itself has been described in many ways, one of which is 'The longest six miles in Jamaica'. In the Blue Mountains section of chapter 5, it is described in terms of the plants and trees you may see as you move up from the trailhead to the Peak. Here, other aspects will be noted. The steepest part of the journey is in the first half, before Portland Gap. Jacob's Ladder, as it has long been named from the former stepping formation, is the steepest stretch of all, but it has now been tarmacked. Soon after that stretch, you come to Portland Gap.

PORTLAND GAP TENT SITE

PORTLAND GAP

There are wooden cabins here with bunks for sleeping, space for tents, and simple sanitary arrangements, including a shower. There is also a tuck shop where you can buy food. If you wish to cook, you have to bring your own food and equipment, but some wood is provided. Sponge mattresses for the bunks can be rented for J$50 a night for residents and US$1 for visitors, you must however supply your own sleeping bags and blankets.

A JCDT ranger is stationed here to assist you and collect fees. It is best to phone JCDT (876-920-8278-9 or 876-960-2848–9) before your arrival so they can give you a booking and the ranger's cell phone number in case of any problems on the way. For details, see appendix.

After Portland Gap, the path is less steep for a while, and you pass through more of the natural forest – trees and ferns, epiphytes, wayside shrubs and herbs. As you climb higher, the vegetation changes and the trees become noticeably shorter.

MOSSES LICHENS AND FERNS

CIGAR BUSH

THE PEAK

At the top there is at present the remains of a vandalised forest shelter, which is still used by walkers although the

Guide to the Blue and John Crow Mountains

THE PEAK   HAPPY CLIMBERS

roof is collapsing.

The views are tremendous if you are not in mist. On a very fine day, with the aid of binoculars, you may be able to see the tops of the Sierra Maestra mountains of southern Cuba. The highest point, where the Trigonometry station stands, is to the right of the flat area where the shelter is.

GORDON TOWN AND HISTORIC TRAILS IN THE PORT ROYAL MOUNTAINS

After following the Hope River gorge from Papine, cross the bridge at Blue Mountain Inn and bear right for Gordon Town. The town probably took its name from the Gordon Highlanders, a British regiment once stationed at Newcastle, or possibly from Dr John Gordon, who, in 1811, purchased the botanic garden originally established here by Hinton East. The garden no longer exists, but – thanks to the botanist James Wiles, who sailed with Captain Bligh – many useful plants were introduced

GORDON TOWN POLICE STATION

57

and nurtured here that are now commonplace.

Before the current road to Newcastle was constructed, Gordon Town was a staging post on the way to Newcastle. The route in use then still serves communities beside the Hope River, joining the main road to Newcastle at Redlight.

TRAIL 1: GORDON TOWN TO REDLIGHT

The trail starts at the well-surfaced road bearing left from the bridge and police station. Vehicles, including minibuses, can go as far as Penfield. The path then winds back and forth across the river, climbing past four waterfalls. Infrastructure along the river is indicative of the importance the route once had. After approximately 1.5 km (0.9 mi) the trail becomes a footpath that splits, the left branch crossing a bridge as it climbs towards Redlight, and the right leading by a pretty trail to Settlement and the Newcastle road about 1 km (0.6 mi) short of Newcastle. Another footpath runs from Redlight to Settlement, to complete the circle. Allow two to two and a half hours for journeying from Gordon Town to Redlight or Settlement.

Because of its accessibility by road and its proximity to several trails, Gordon Town is a good place to start a hike. Overlooked by the police station, the square is safe, and it has space for parking vehicles. It could be worth the extra time and effort to climb the police station steps and let the duty officer know your plans before you set off.

SOAPWOOD

FLORA RIVER

© HERMAN TOBISCH

Guide to the Blue and John Crow Mountains

The Park and its Surroundings

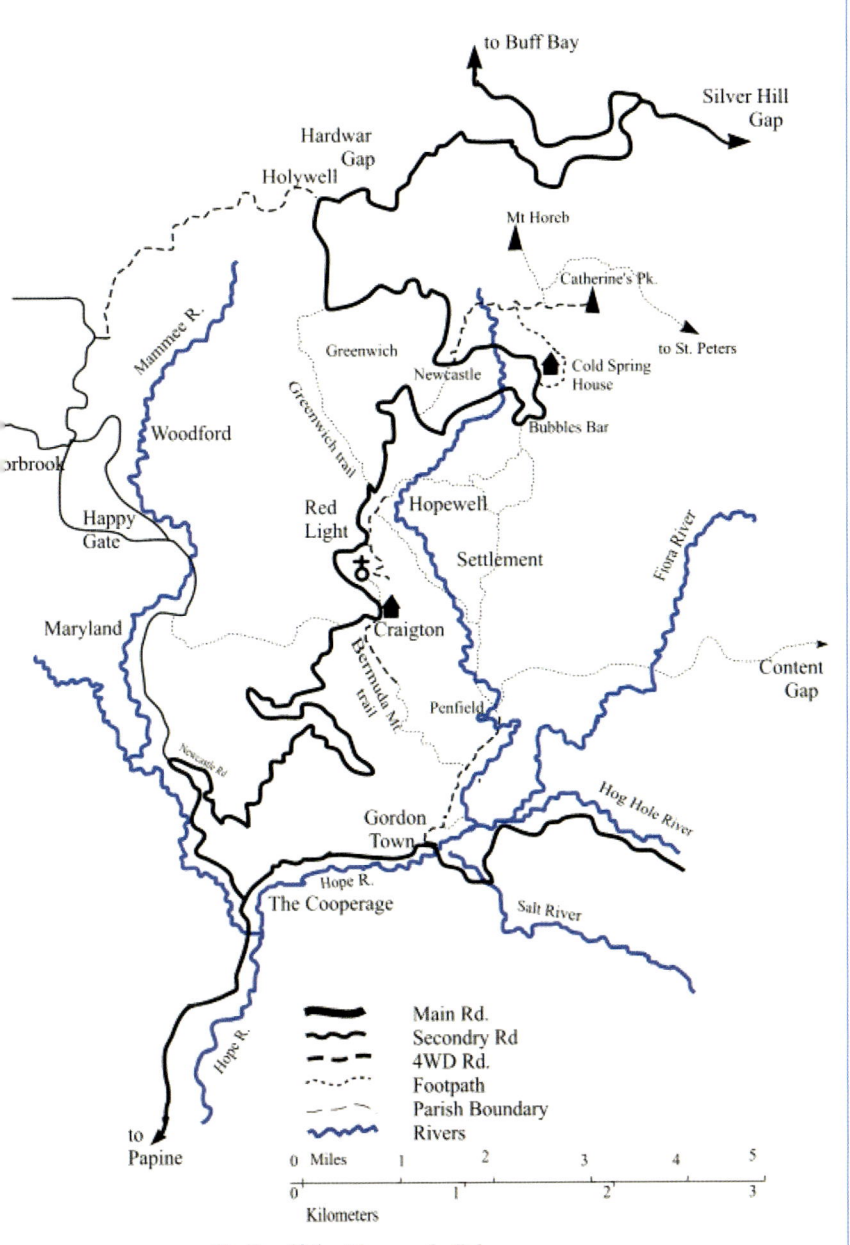

Trails off the Newcastle Rd.
and connecting with Gordon Town

TRAIL 2: GORDON TOWN TO CONTENT GAP (KNOWN AS SUGARLOAF TRAIL)

A narrow bridge to the right at Penfield leads to a path that was once a major route to Content Gap. It is prone to landslides during storms but is usually maintained by local farmers. However, storm damage has resulted in the path being very steep in places with a loose surface. It follows closely the Flora River. There are some pretty waterfalls and an old stone bridge with weep-holes to allow flood waters to flow over it. Further on you will come to a wooden bridge. The path becomes steep as it leads through high grass, after which there are a few smallholdings. Veer right for Content Gap. As this section may be overgrown it is best to enquire about its condition from the homes alongside the river. Allow one and a half to two hours for the walk.

TRAIL 3: BERMUDA MOUNT TRAIL

This trail has excellent views of Gordon Town and the surrounding hills. It starts a short distance above the Gordon

GORDON TOWN BELOW

Town post office, beginning by a gatepost incised with the name 'Rawcliffe'. It reaches the main road to Newcastle at Craighton beside the Ueshima coffee farm. The walk takes about an hour and a half.

IPOMOEA

GORDON TOWN TO GUAVA RIDGE INTERSECTION

For Guava Ridge, 11 km (about 7 mi) from Gordon Town, cross the bridge beside the police station and proceed uphill. Several steep, narrow roads and tracks meet the road before it reaches Guava Ridge. Most of those to the right of the main roadway eventually lead to Flamstead, a lookout post as far back as the days of the Taino.

TRAIL 4: FOOT TRAIL TO FLAMSTEAD

Starting 800 m (0.5 mi) above Gordon Town, on the right-hand side, there is a steep trail just beyond the house of Milling Spring, where water passes under the road. It meets a rough driving road opposite an anthurium nursery under shade cloth. That road, Coffee Walk, leaves the Gordon Town main road 800 m (0.5 mi) further up, as the second steep paved road

PORT ROYAL MOUNTAINS, EUCALYPTUS TREES

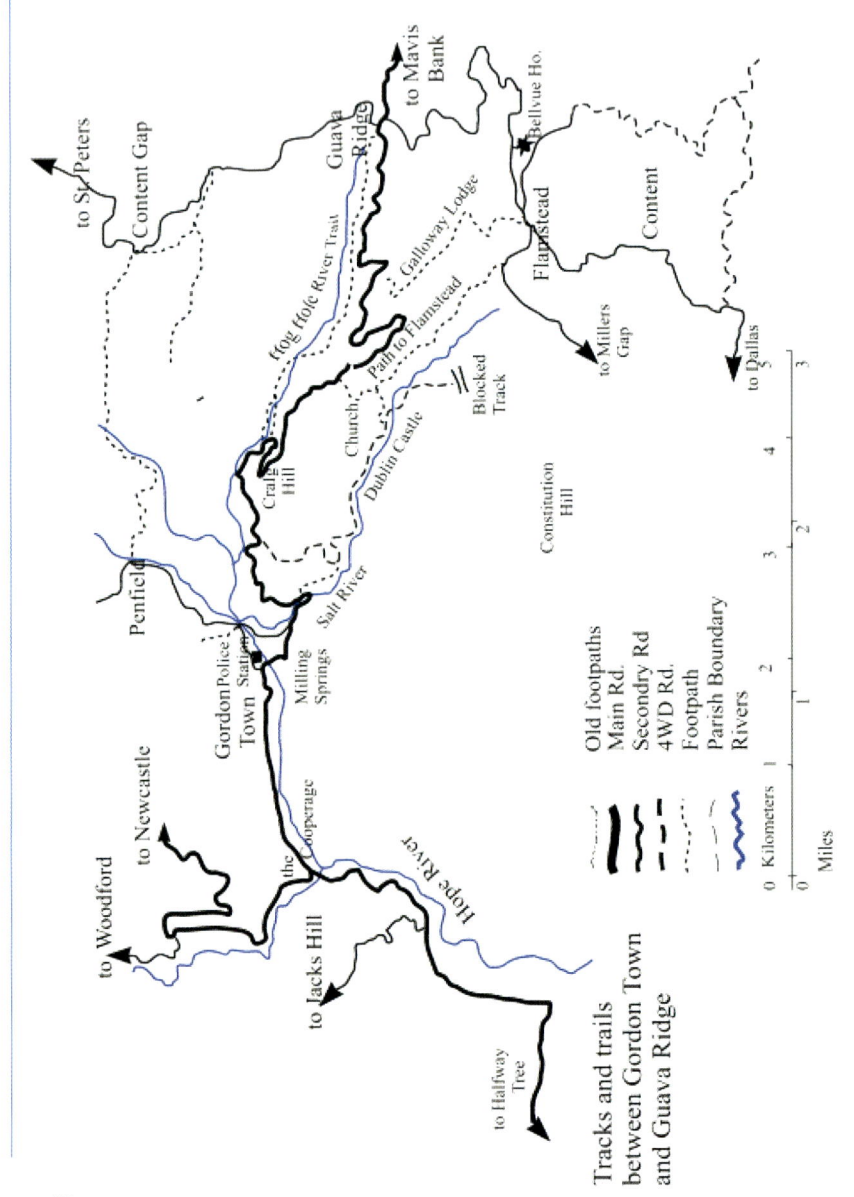

Tracks and trails between Gordon Town and Guava Ridge

on the right. The surface quickly deteriorates. Follow it uphill to the community of Dublin Castle, sprawling along a valley. A trail to the left, beside the Church of the First Born (you will need to ask for it), used to be the main route to Flamstead. The path borders a valley and follows a water pipe. This challenging walk to above 1,300 m (4,000 ft), through changing vegetation and interesting views, takes four hours. It is joined by a rough driving road, 7.4 km (4.6 mi) from Gordon Town on the way to Guava Ridge, just before the multicoloured building on your left called World's End.

STRIPE HEADED TANAGER

TRAIL 5: HOGHOLE RIVER TRAIL

Craig Hill is 2.9 km (1.8 mi) from Gordon Town. Here, on a sharp corner with a flowing water catchment, is a parochial road that goes straight ahead beside some factory buildings. It follows the Hoghole River as a footpath to Guava Ridge. Near some old farm buildings, it crosses the steep farm road leading down from the main road. At the bottom a track crosses the Hoghole River and, before reaching the steep hill of the farm, passes through the stone remains of a once large coffee pulpery. This track continues to Guava Ridge. The trail may not be passable except by walking in the river.

SHOEBLACK HIBISCUS

TRAIL 6: GALLOWAY LODGE TRAIL

Above the main road, just before the Petersfield sign 10 km (6.25 mi) from Gordon Town, is the Galloway Lodge road to Flamstead. There are two roads here. Take the one that comes off at an angle almost parallel to the main road. The quaint old house of Galloway Lodge is to the right of the track. The path to it goes through juniper trees and is not easy to find. There is also a large stand of juniper trees at the beginning of this road. Along the bank of the main road, look for begonias, red salvia and, during December and January, tiny red Achimenes in damp spots.

Four roads worth exploring meet at Guava Ridge, where there are several makeshift shops. Jerk chicken is the Friday specialty.

RED SALVIA
© JILL BYLES

TRAIL 7: GOVERNOR'S BENCH TRAIL, BELLEVUE GREAT HOUSE AND FLAMSTEAD

Turning right (south) at Guava Ridge takes you onto a scenic road, first to one end of the trail variously called Governor's Bench and Mt Rosanna trail, then to Bellevue Great House, a 300-year-old coffee estate house now owned by the University of the West Indies, and on to Flamstead.

On the last steep right bend before reaching the Bellevue house, a track leads left past a house named 'Above Concerns'. The track runs along a ridge overlooking the sea with views of the Palisadoes, Port Royal and the cays. It ends in two footpaths that run precariously along the hillside and then along

GOVERNOR'S BENCH TRAIL
© H. TOBISCH

64 Guide to the Blue and John Crow Mountains

The Park and its Surroundings

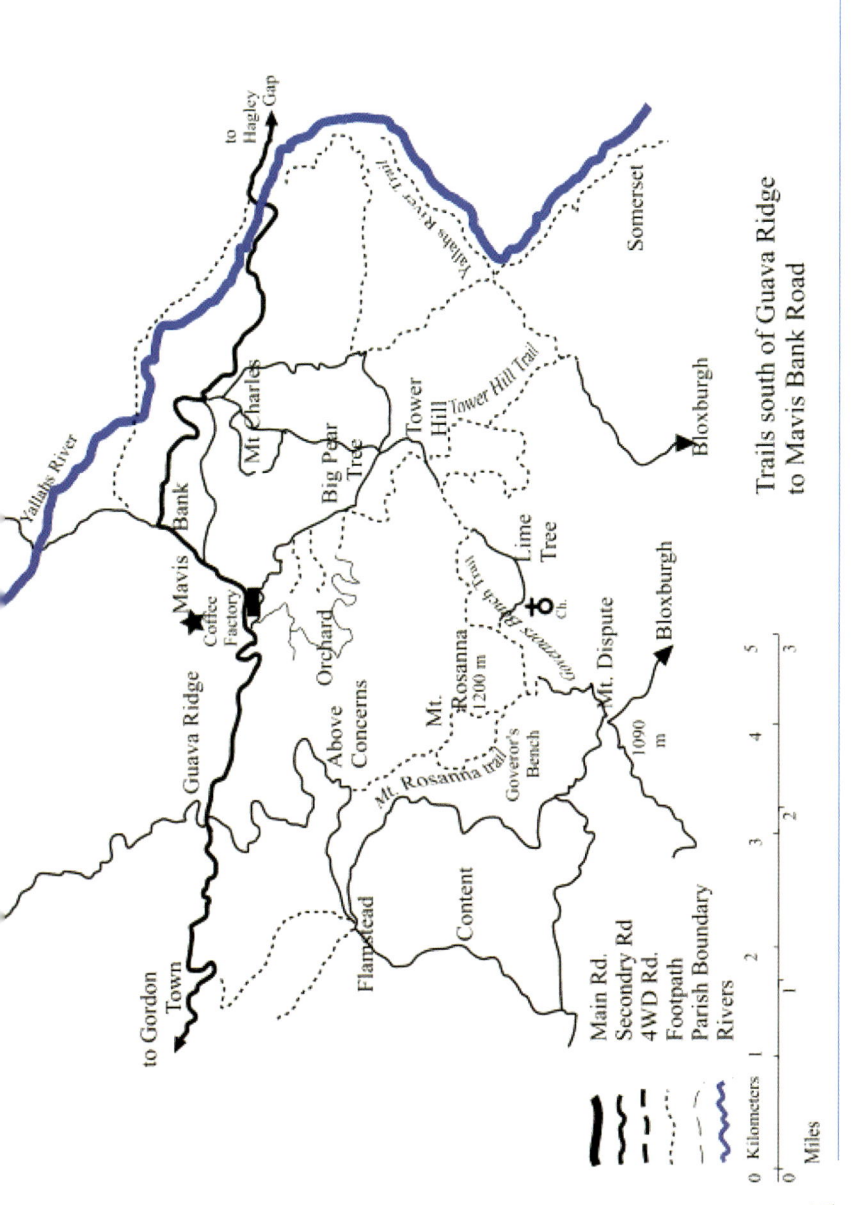

65

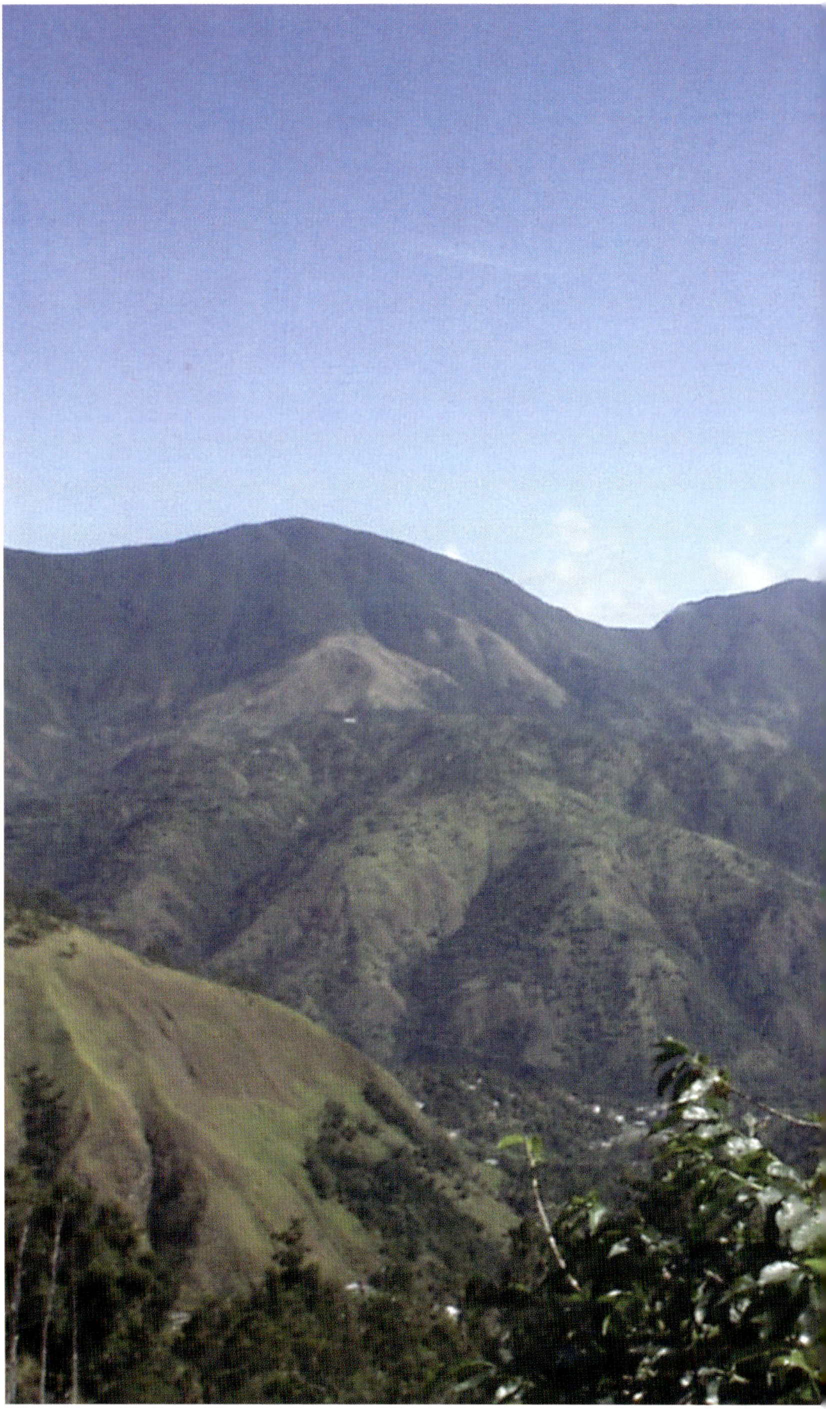

The Parks and its Surroundings

BLUE MOUNTAIN PEAK FROM BELLEVUE ROAD

© JILL BYLES

a knife-edge ridge to Mount Rosanna (1,300 m; 4,000 ft), where there are great views in all directions. The trail leads south to Governor's Bench, and then to Limetree (see next section for approaches from Mavis Bank to Limetree). In 2004 hurricane Ivan blew eucalyptus trees across the track so the traveller had to climb under then over the trunks in order to reach the end of the ridge. Here small footpaths pass each side of the mound to join into one leading up to the top of Mount Rosanna, 1300 m, 4000 ft. This stands high above the surrounding country with views in all directions. A steep track leads down from here to Limetree.

PALISADOES FROM PORT ROYAL MOUNTAINS

Returning to the road from Guava Ridge, continue uphill to Bellevue Great House on the left and on past the house belonging to the Manley family, two of whom were prime ministers of Jamaica. Edna Manley's sculpture is internationally known. The road leads to Flamstead Square, where five roads meet. On the right is the road to Galloway Lodge and the Guava Ridge town road, and next is the road leading to the Flamstead trail from Dublin Castle (both already described). The road from Bellevue continues to Flamstead Hill, where bilberry and juniper are found. To the left of the square is a road down through coffee farms, past the remains of Good Hope Great House. Trails from it go up to Mount Dispute and down to the coast, or to the foothills behind Papine.

FLAMSTEAD

Flamstead Hill was used in Taino times as a lookout, and also by the Spanish and the British navies, because it affords a good view of the coastline and the approaches to Port Royal and Kingston Harbour. It was here that the first chronometer, an instrument used to determine longitude at sea, was tested and found to be accurate. Flamstead was named after the Royal Naval Observatory's Flamstead House at Greenwich. Its

The Park and its Surroundings

ARTHROSTEMA FRAGILE

significance as a strategic site continued into World War II.

Instead of going to Flamstead Hill past the radio mast, you can pass the attractive houses on the right and take a track down to Content and Ross's Valley, where several trails reach districts on the hills to the south. Then take the steep Good Hope road up to Flamstead Square. Or you can take a short walk down to Content and turn left, to come up almost opposite the entrance to the ruins of Flamstead House.

Flamstead was a fashionable resort for the governors of Jamaica, their families and military and naval officers. As a guesthouse, Flamstead was known throughout the Caribbean until the mid-twentieth century. Most of the building was demolished in 1988 by hurricane Gilbert. To relive the history, ask in the square for Mr Robinson, once the caretaker. There is a Flamstead Heritage Society through which tours can be arranged. Attractive homes nearby can be rented for short stays. Contact oledog@colis.com to rent Honey Hill. For more about the Flamstead area, see the very detailed Flamstead Web site.

TOWER HILL AND LIMETREE

The Tower Hill road branches off the Mavis Bank road, fords the Fall River and passes the coffee factory gates. Continue straight ahead. Some large gates on the left of the Tower Hill road are the entrance to a coffee farm. A shaded track leads through the farm to paths to Mt Charles, the Yallahs River crossing and Tower Hill. Opposite the gates are short forest trails sometimes used by birdwatchers. A longer one, higher up the road, to the right of a steep bend, passes a small waterfall.

Beside the bar/shop in Tower Hill, a track can be seen going along a ridge, past the Postal Agency, to some houses. From it, Mavis Bank and the surrounding hills and valleys appear laid out like a relief map. The path is narrow, leading steeply down.

TREE FERNS

ON THE TRAIL

It meets a better-defined track that goes from Big Pear Tree to a junction, where the left track goes to Mt Charles and the right track through a gate to skirt a large coffee and poultry farm. It comes to a huge, unfinished, stone water tank before descending to the Yallahs River crossing and the route to Hagley Gap. Both routes are very steep. There is also a track from the poultry farm along the Yallahs River to Somerset.

The road ends at Limetree, beyond Tower Hill. There is a guesthouse at Limetree Farm (876-881-8788). Towards the right, beside the church, is the track that goes to Mount Rosanna, Governor's Bench and Bellevue, or to Mount Dispute.

THE SOUTHERN APPROACHES: THE BLUE MOUNTAIN FOOTHILLS FROM ST. THOMAS

THE RAMBLE ROAD

After Bull Bay, on the coast road through St. Thomas from Kingston, there is a turning inland at Eleven Mile. It is a remote road over Cambridge Hill, through dry forest, with good sea views. There are unpaved roads off it leading to a quarry

JUDGMENT CLIFF

BLUE MOUNTAINS FROM ST. THOMAS

below. At Llandewey it merges with a road from Easington to the right, which starts where the Yallahs River enters the sea, and just before Llandewey is a view of Judgment Cliff. If you miss the Eleven Mile road, you will find the road to Easington from the coast road well marked, as it has to be used if the coast road is flooded at the Yallahs fording.

Judgment Cliff was named after the great earthquake in 1692, which caused a goodly part of Port Royal to disappear under the sea. Here in St Thomas, a large part of Mt Sinai split

71

Southern Approaches

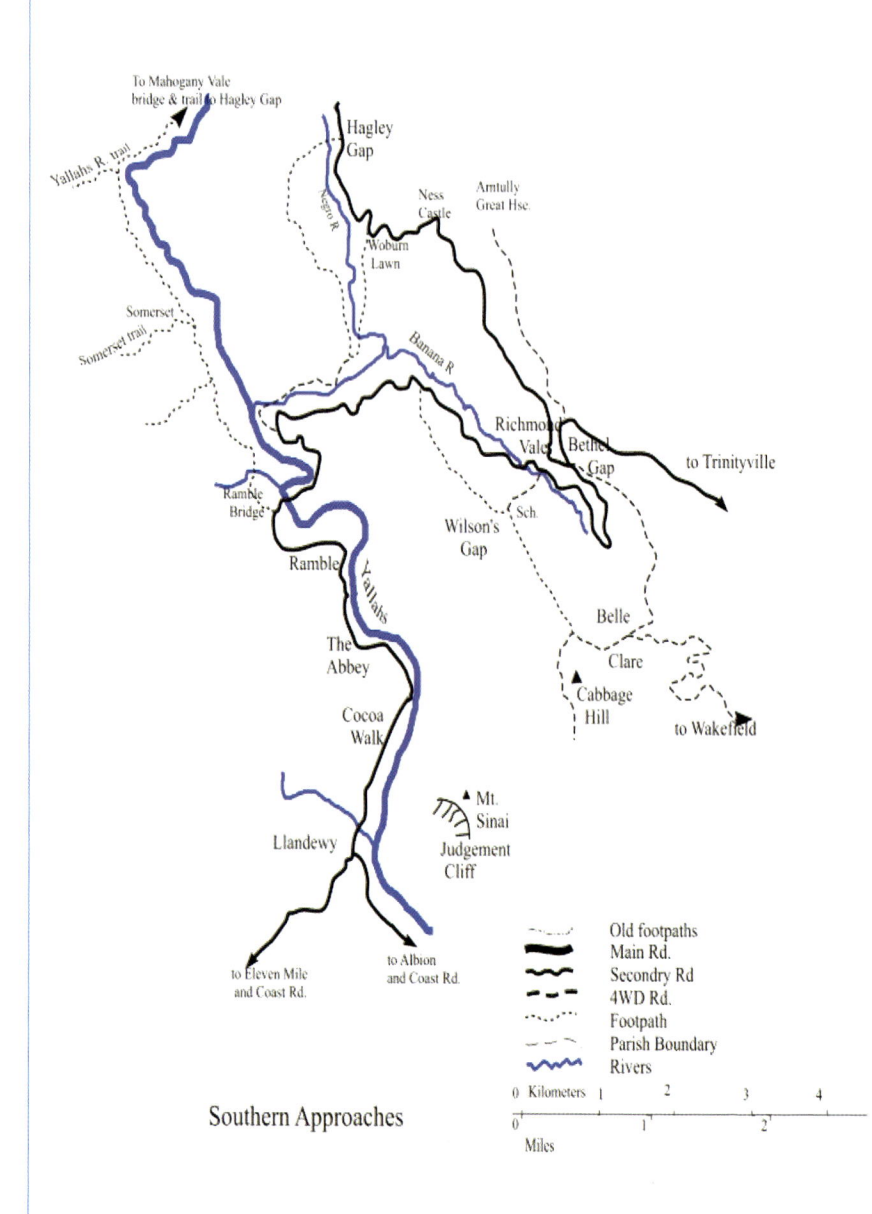

Guide to the Blue and John Crow Mountains

The Park and its Surroundings

BRIDGE AT RAMBLE

off and slid down to crush and bury the property that lay below – and its owner, a Dutch planter who was regarded locally as a wicked man. The scarred hillside and mound remains as a landmark.

After merging, the road continues beside the Yallahs, meandering through coffee farms via Cocoa Walk to Ramble, where the Shooting River meets the Yallahs. Here a bridge crosses high above the narrow Yallahs River gorge. Beside the bridge, a track runs down left; it reaches Somerset, where several trails meet, serving people in the southern hills. The high road continues beside the Yallahs River as far as Windsor Forest. There are several views of the Yallahs River pipeline, which supplies water to parts of the Corporate Area. The road turns east at Finger Post, where a left turning drops down to the Negro River, which meets the Yallahs. This road goes as far as the nearby community of River Head, after which it becomes a track leading to Hagley Gap via Kerrick Hill and Lady's View. It is clearly defined, especially from the high points. The main road climbs through Richmond Vale, where there is a Baptist church, one of the original stone buildings erected around 1830. At one time it was used for processing coffee. There is also a wooden administrative building, constructed around 1920.

The next community is Bethel Gap, where there is a junction. Keep left for Hagley Gap near Bethel Gap and right for Cedar Valley and the road to Morant Bay.

LOOKING SOUTH FROM RAMBLE BRIDGE

THE BAPTIST CHURCH IN JAMAICA

The Baptists hold a very special place in Jamaican history. In the late eighteenth and early nineteenth centuries, they brought their mission to the black community, whose members had been excluded from church and school by the white authorities. They introduced the concept of equality by teaching that the one God was the spiritual father of black and white, that he was a loving God and could be reached by prayer. By teaching from the Bible and introducing hymn books, they introduced literacy. Churches sprang up at places such as Richmond Vale and Stony Gut, near Morant Bay. Indirectly, the Baptists inspired three of Jamaica's National Heroes: Sam Sharpe, the slave who led the Kensington anti-slavery uprising in 1831; Deacon Bogle of Stony Gut, who led the Morant Bay rebellion; and George William Gordon, another Baptist deacon but also an elected member of the Assembly, a Justice of the Peace, a landowner and businessman, and a friend of Bogle. All three were executed, the latter two hanged with many others after the rebellion in 1864. There is a statue of Bogle by Edna Manley which stands in the square in Morant Bay.

MORANT BAY COURTHOUSE

BETHEL GAP AND ALBION MOUNTAIN

At Bethel Gap there is a steep road that goes south to the radio mast on Cabbage Hill, at the top of Albion Mountain. Here there are breathtaking views of the coast and the John Crow Mountains. It is particularly beautiful here on moonlit nights, when the mountains can be seen silhouetted against the sky. There are coffee farms on the way but the area is sparsely populated nowadays, as there are few amenities. Several varieties of orchids, ferns and bromeliads populate the embankments, along with escaped ornamentals. At Belle Clare, on the way up to Cabbage Hill from Bethel Gap, the road is joined by another road going east through Mount Vernon, where it runs beside the White River to Trinityville. Yet another road descends steeply northwest to Richmond Vale, through Wilson Gap. Here, on the sharp corner before the descent to Richmond Vale, there is a bar/shop with friendly people and a seat in the shade. Rest awhile and then walk or drive uphill to the small school with its magnificent view. Trails once returned to the Yallahs River from here.

SUNDAY MORNING

VIEW OVER YALLAHS

Passing the turn-off to the transmitters on Cabbage Hill, the road narrows. There are some abandoned dwellings, and at Upper Mount Vernon, at the end of the driving road, is an isolated bar (probably closed). Beside it, a track follows the White River to Trinityville via the Mount Vernon school, where it joins the road from Belle Clare.

TRINITYVILLE AND CEDAR VALLEY

Trinityville is also accessible by either of two roads turning inland from the main coast road, one on each side of the Morant River. One starts from Belvedere on the west side, and the

BLUE MOUNTAINS FROM MORANT RIVER

SPANISH ELM FLOWERING

other from Morant Bay on the east. The latter is the better road; it runs through flat farmland, past Seaforth and the Serge Island Dairies to Trinityville, once a prosperous and fashionable town, thanks to sugar. The road passes a factory for the processing of ackees, and there is an ackee orchard further on, with an old stone building on the property. On the other side of Trinityville, a road crosses the river on the right. It goes to Somerset and Shirley Castle

The Park and its Surroundings

FOOTHILLS FROM TRINITYVILLE

CEDAR VALLEY POLICE STATION

on Morgan's River. A lot of coffee is grown in this area. At cooler Cedar Valley, at the foot of the Blue Mountains range close to the Negro River, there are anthurium nurseries under shade cloth. The stone house on the corner, now the local police station and administrative offices, suggests that the area was once more stylish. A rocky, coffee-lined road to the right passes the Moy Hall coffee factory, and the privately owned old estate house of Arntully is at the end. For Hagley Gap, take the road to the left and then sharp right, which goes through Bethel Gap, Woburn Lawn and Ness Castle, where a footpath by the school is a link to Arntully.

HAGLEY GAP

Beyond Bethel Gap, towards Hagley Gap, most of the road has never been paved. A low-slung vehicle is not advisable,

RAMGOAT DASHLONG

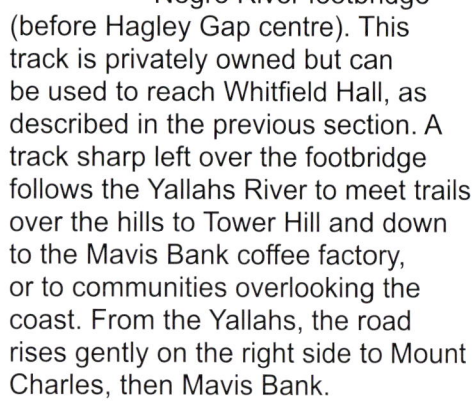

NIGHT BLOOMING CACTUS BEFORE DAWN

AGAVE FLOWER

especially as there are two fords to be crossed before reaching Hagley Gap. Particular caution is advised at the one just below Hagley Gap, especially after rain. Hagley Gap and the communities above may be marooned when the Yallahs and Negro rivers are high. Some coffee grows along this section of the road, but there is little sign of the lush vegetation associated with the Blue Mountains.

A track to the left before Hagley Gap is the one over Kerrick Hill that leads to the Ramble road. The road to Blue Mountain Peak ascends from the centre of Hagley Gap, and the road downhill from the centre leads to the Yallahs River at Mahogany Vale. A track leads to the Old Radnor coffee estate from the Negro River footbridge (before Hagley Gap centre). This track is privately owned but can be used to reach Whitfield Hall, as described in the previous section. A track sharp left over the footbridge follows the Yallahs River to meet trails over the hills to Tower Hill and down to the Mavis Bank coffee factory, or to communities overlooking the coast. From the Yallahs, the road rises gently on the right side to Mount Charles, then Mavis Bank.

The Park and its Surroundings

THE EASTERN SECTION

BATH AND THE MOUNTAINS

From the coast road through St. Thomas, several roads lead to Bath, nestling close to the mountains. All of them are potholed, and the journey will take much longer than anticipated. From Kingston, the most direct route is by turning inland at Morant Bay. Look for large-leafed teak trees near the approaches to the Plantain Garden River, and on the road's rock embankment there are Pitcairnias – bromeliads with long, tapering, serrated leaves and spikes of red flowers. A slightly better drive is by way of the crossroads at Hordley, a mile beyond Golden Grove, after leaving Morant Bay. The road is straight and flat and follows the Plantain Garden River through cane and bananas.

TRAILS ACROSS THE MOUNTAINS FROM BATH

Two trails cross the Blue Mountains near Bath. One, yet to be reopened, starts at the bottom of the hill leading to the Fountain and crosses the John Crows via Corn Puss Gap to Bowden Pen, approximately 16 km (10 mi) away on the Rio Grande, which rises close to the trail and forms the border between the parishes of St. Thomas and Portland. Much of the forest through which the trail passes is primary rain forest. There are trees with such local names as soapwood, breakaxe and bloodwood. There are also the Santa Maria and cedar and the water mahoe, the food of the Jamaican Giant Swallowtail butterfly (*Pterourus homerus*, formerly *Papilio homerus*), which may be seen after periods of rain. Bowden Pen and the once flourishing banana port of Bowden, near Port Morant, were once part of the same property. For a reliable guide to this trail, ask in Bath

JOHN CROW BUSH

WALKERS ON CUNA CUNA PASS TRAIL

79

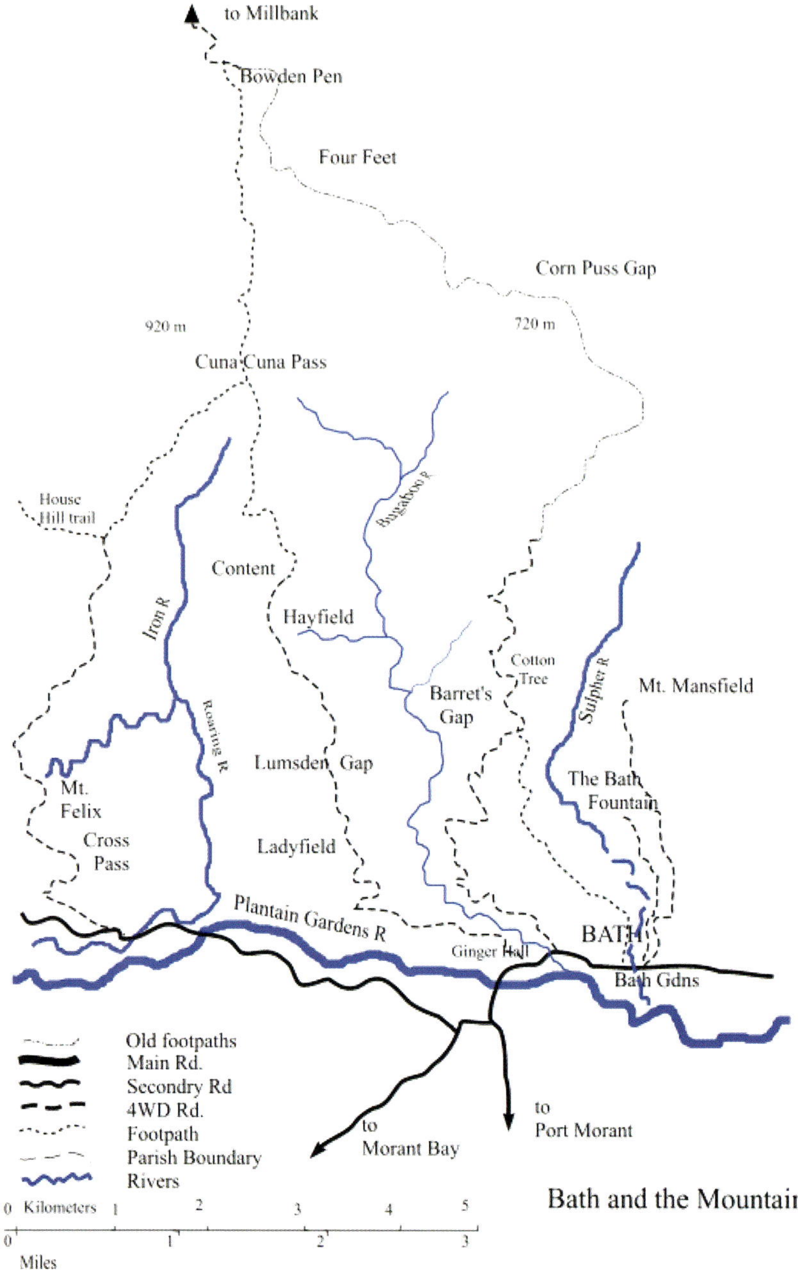

Bath and the Mountains

The Park and its Surroundings

VIEW FROM CUNA CUNA PASS TRAIL

COMMON ROOM

CABIN AT BOWDEN PEN

for Mr Reboe, or contact Heritage Tours or Ms Linette Wilks (see appendix for details).

The shorter trail of 11 km (7 mi) crosses the Cuna Cuna Pass. This is where the mountain chain is at its narrowest. To the west of the pass is the Blue Mountain range, and to the east stretch the John Crow Mountains. This trail to Bowden Pen (Four Feet) is now being well maintained. It starts at Hayfield, a 6.4 km (4 mi) drive from Bath. The steep road to Hayfield starts near Bath, at Ginger Hall, close to the bridge over the Plantain Garden River. There is a climb of 430 m (1,410 ft) from Hayfield through disturbed vegetation to the Cuna Cuna Pass, called 'Lookout' because there are views of St Thomas on one side and Portland on the other. To the left of the climb is the Iron River, and across its valley is House Hill, where an eighteenth-century house once stood. The left fork at Lookout goes to House Hill and joins a road back to the Plantain Garden River.

This trail is only partially clear at present. The forest of the Cuna Cuna Pass is less intact than that of Corn Puss Gap, and there are many introduced species including bamboo, wild banana, ginger lilies, dasheen and yam as well as fruit trees. A steep, slippery track to the right off the well-defined trail leads down to Quaco Falls, significant in Maroon history. Also on the right, a short distance further on, is a narrow trail down through a grove of rose apples, distorted by the weight of the twisted, rope-like stems of a cacoon vine, Entada gigas (*Mimoseaceae*). The pods can be a metre or more long, and the shiny, brown seeds up to 7 cm across. The trail veers right to Bowden Pen and the unpaved road to Milbank. At Bowden Pen there are comfortable rustic cabins, and with prior notice food can be prepared for you. To arrange a package which includes a guided hike, contact Linette Wilks, a Maroon from Bowden Pen, tel 876-395-5351. For more about Ms Wilks and the area, see the section below

81

BATH AND THE BATH GARDENS

The town of Bath, which grew up around hot sulphur springs that were discovered to have curative powers by a runaway slave in 1690, has very little to show of its former prosperity. The forest spring cured the slave's leg ulcers, and he returned to his master with the news. After the government bought and promoted the spring in 1699, the town that sprung up around it became The Bath of St. Thomas the Apostle, the most fashionable place in Jamaica.

BATH GARDENS GROUNDS

Thomas Clarke, physician to the baths, experimented with camphor, tea, litchi and sago palm in 1774. This led to the establishment of a botanical garden in 1779. Plants from overseas that were established at Bath included breadfruit, brought from Tahiti on Captain Bligh's second voyage; ackee, mango, cinnamon, pandanus and others, captured from a Haiti-bound French ship by one of Lord Rodney's ships in the Indian Ocean. They were grown at Bath, and then young plants were distributed around the island.

The garden had a history of ups and downs. It was prone to flooding, and it was never allocated sufficient funds. Dr James Macfayden, who became Island Botanist in 1826, experimented with local plants there and later published *A Flora of Jamaica*. After he left, the garden experienced lean times again. It was rescued in 1847 by Nathaniel Wilson of Kew Gardens. He experimented with cinchona, known to relieve the symptoms of malaria. As Bath Gardens were too small and the altitude too low, the project was continued in the Blue Mountains in 1868. By the end of the century there were gardens at Hope, Castleton and Cinchona in the Blue Mountains, and Bath was in decline again. The town itself became a ghost town after the Morant Bay uprising of 1864.

Several well-seasoned exotic trees are what remain of the botanical gardens. Perhaps the largest is a Barringtonia, with seedpods like a tasselled bishop's mitre. Along the roadside approaching the town are some unusual plants and some naturalised fruit trees, including the Breadfruit, Otaheite apple and Rose apple, which flourish in the damp conditions of the mountain valleys and bear witness to the former glory of the gardens.

The Bath Fountain Hotel, with its hot and cold springs, is open to the public. Tel 876-703-4154 or 876-703-4345. Room rates are modest. There is also a restaurant. Across the river and behind the hotel is a pleasant walk up beside Sulphur River. There are delicate ferns, pileas, Piperaceae and Melastomaceae among the plants lining the bank. During the winter months there may be also tiny red-flowered Achimenes. Peripatus is found here in moist areas (see chapter 6, The Invertebrates).

ROSE APPLE

ACKEE

BREADFRUIT

BARRINGTONIA SEED PODS AND FLOWERS

and the section on the Rio Grande Valley.

FROM BOWDEN PEN

From Bowden Pen, 2.4 km (1.5 mi) along the road towards Milbank there is a wide path joining it from the left. This is the end of the Cuna Cuna trail.

VIEW FROM CUNA CUNA PASS

Yellow-billed and the much less common Black-billed Parrots may be heard or seen in the John Crow Mountains. Also listen for cawing from the Jabbering Crows. Notice that the Streamertail hummingbirds of the Bath area and further east have black bills, whereas in the remainder of the island they have red bills.

Do not attempt these trails without a recommended guide. Walking in the John Crow Mountains can be dangerous. Some parts have rarely been penetrated by humans, and the honeycomb rock is pitted with jagged holes. Even clearly defined trails can be treacherous when wet. Feral hogs, hunted by men and dogs for their meat, inhabit the forest.

JOHN CROWS FROM BOWDEN

The Maroons used the trails linking Bath to Millbank in the Rio Grande Valley as escape routes to their established settlements such as Moore Town. After the Maroon Treaty of 1739, the governor ordered the routes to be kept open.

LOOKING SOUTH FROM JOHNSON MOUNTAIN

Guide to the Blue and John Crow Mountains

THE EASTERN SLOPES OF THE JOHN CROW MOUNTAINS

JOHNSON MOUNTAIN

Some 8 km (5 mi) east of Bath is the small settlement of Wheelersfield, from which a road climbs to Johnson Mountain. There are wonderful views of the south and eastern coast lands from the upper sections of the road. From Johnson Mountain village, an old forestry road leads upward through rain forest to within sight of the ramparts of the southern edge of the John Crow Mountains.

Many of the plants described in the John Crow section of chapter 4, on the flora, can be seen from this trail. At the top a forest of blue mahoe is seen, reaching to the edge of the ramparts.

If you are fortunate, you will also see the magnificent Jamaican Giant Swallowtail butterfly (*Pterourus homerus*, formerly *Papilio homerus*) serenely flying over the small streams by the path. Its larval food plant, the water mahoe, grows well in the area.

PACKI RIVER TO BIG LEVEL

BLUE MAHOE

BLUE MAHOE FLOWER

Packi River is in Portland, near the St Thomas border. It is best approached by the good road from Grange Hill. Bear left to the Packi River ford and walk from this point. The road ahead leads to Haining and is worth exploring, but a road nearby leads to a water catchment where a clear limestone pond is shaded by a huge ficus tree, from which, when last seen, hung several large, untidy Jamaican Becards' nests. At that time a pair of Becards was in the process of constructing their nest. Becards (see chapter 8, 'The Birds') build nests up to a metre in length from dried grass, leaves, ferns, moss and so forth. The road to the water catchment continues upward to a view of Big

PHILODENDRON

MOUNTAIN CABBAGE PALM

FLOWER OF MOUNTAIN CABBAGE

Level, a part of the John Crow Mountain top. The forest on either side is secondary growth, and much of that is degraded up to a certain point. The undergrowth is a mass of several varieties of thick-stemmed, fleshy-leaved philodendrons, which also cover many of the trees. The stems are used to weave baskets and furniture. Underfoot is fossilised coral; this area was once a living coral reef beneath the sea. The shells of various species of snails are scattered amongst the leaf litter, and there is the occasional shiny millipede up to 10 cm (4 in) long. You may be surprised to find a hermit crab, or 'soldier', inhabiting one of these snail shells, or even one carrying a seashell on its back. Some soldiers carry their homes up to 500 m (550 yds) and higher.

Keep following the track right, and after about 1.5 km (0.9 mi) the forest shows signs of recovery, closing in on the path, which leads to a gorge with a stream at the bottom and the remains of an aqueduct. Above the gorge are panoramic views of the coast and Big Level, heavily forested. A distant hillside is dotted with the white flowers of the wild frangipani (*Plumeria obtusa*). Look for the endemic tree called anchovy pear (*Grias cauliflora*). It has leaves up to a metre (3.2 ft) long and 20 cm (about 8 in) across, which hang in clusters towards the ends of the branches. It grows in wet areas – for example, Portland and the Black River swamp. There are also many specimens of the endemic royal palm or

86 Guide to the Blue and John Crow Mountains

The Park and its Surroundings

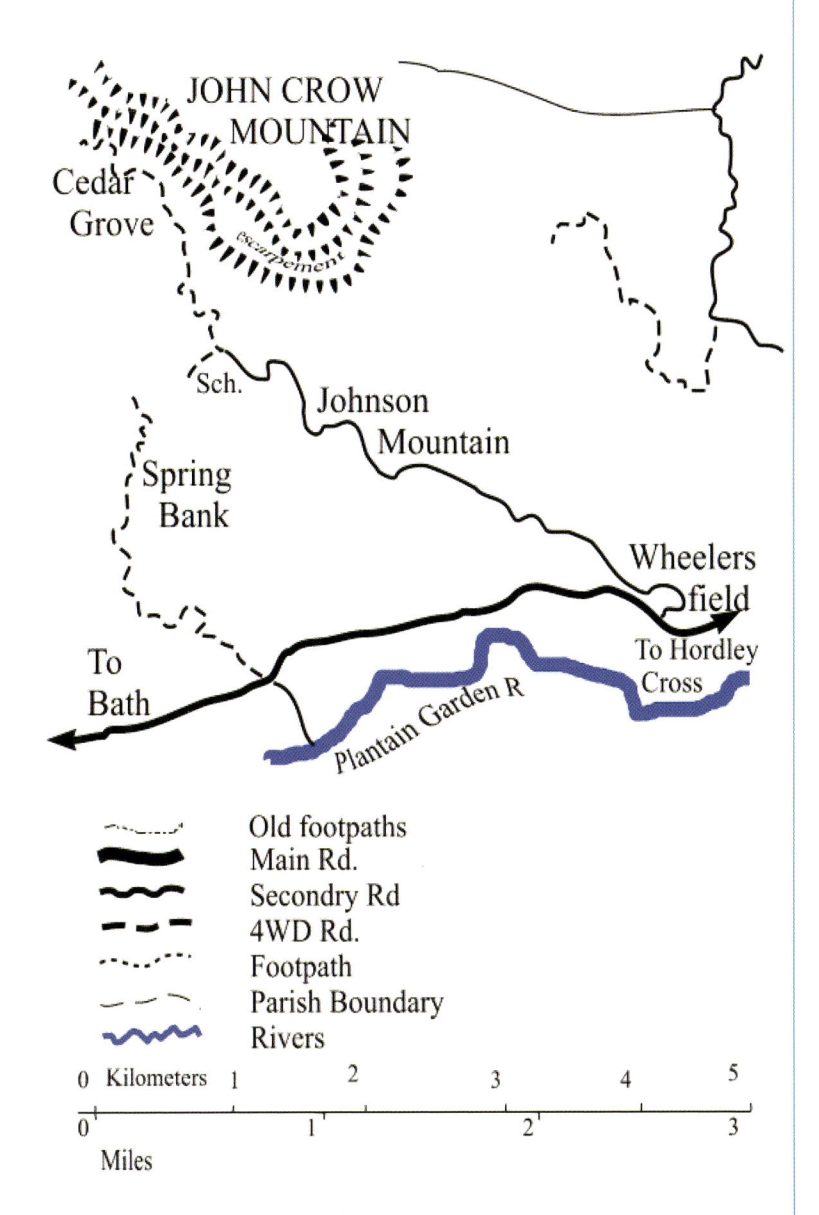

JOHN CROW MOUNTAIN

Cedar Grove

escarpement

Sch.

Johnson Mountain

Spring Bank

Wheelers field

To Bath

To Hordley Cross

Plantain Garden R.

- Old footpaths
- Main Rd.
- Secondry Rd.
- 4WD Rd.
- Footpath
- Parish Boundary
- Rivers

Kilometers 0 1 2 3 4 5

Miles 0 1 2 3

Johnson Mountain

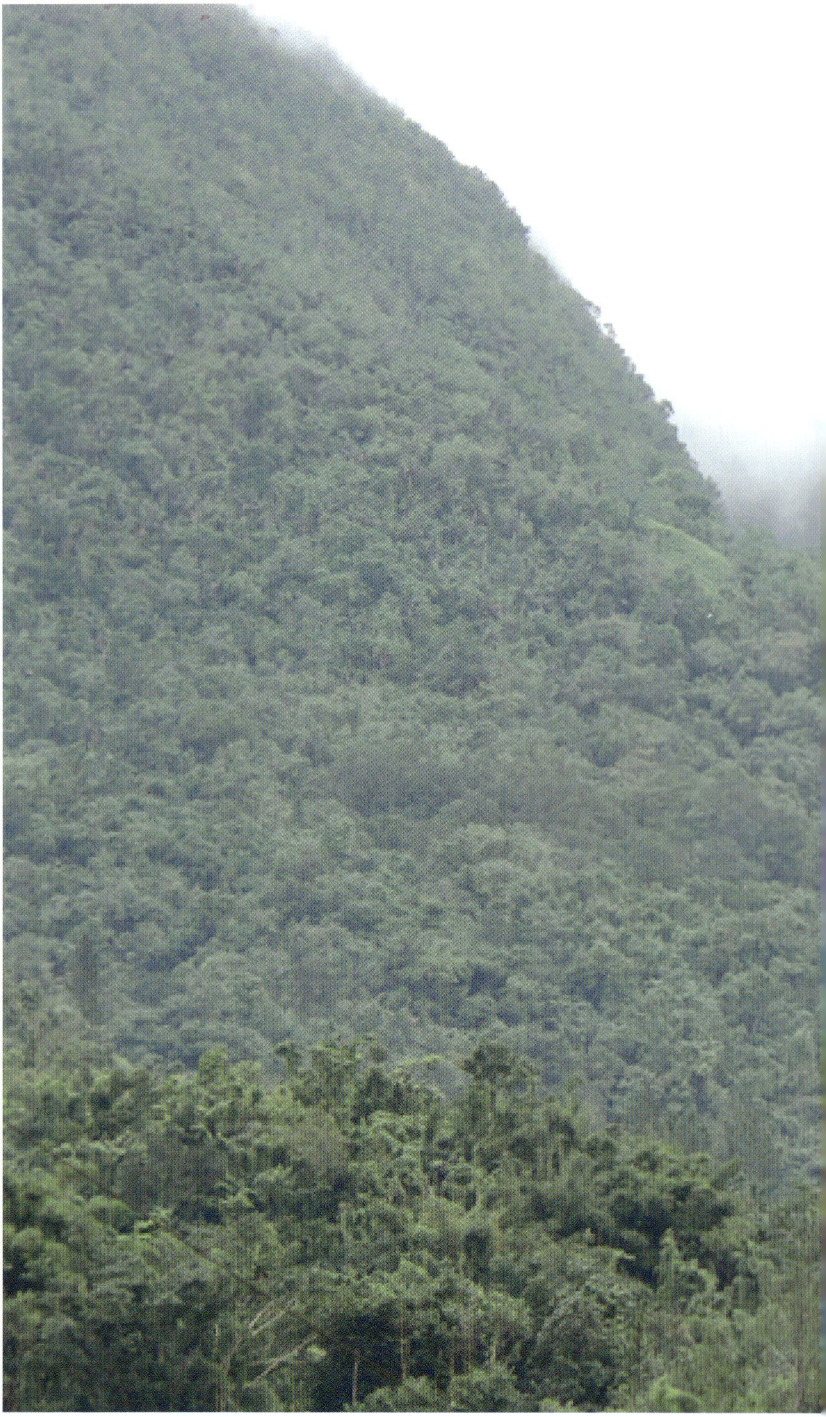

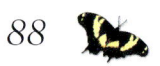

The Park and its Surroundings

JOHN CROW MOUNTAINS

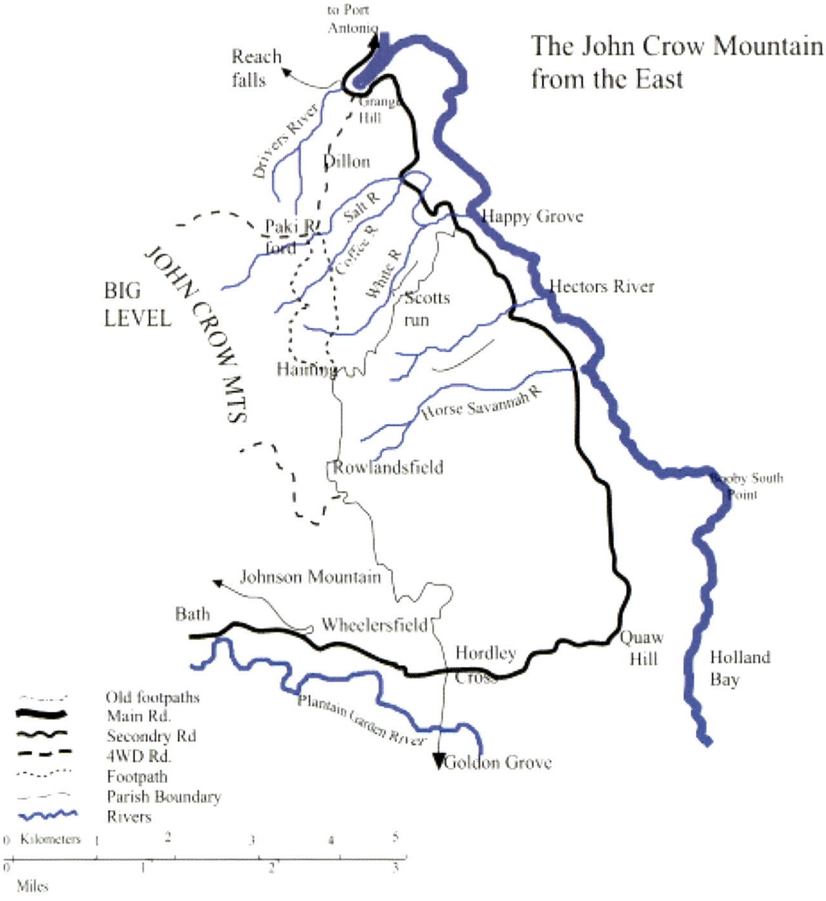
The John Crow Mountain from the East
to Port Antonio
Reach falls
Drivers River
Dillon
Paki R ford
Salt R
Coffee R
White R
Happy Grove
Hectors River
Scotts run
BIG LEVEL
JOHN CROW MTS
Horse Savannah R
Rowlandsfield
Johnson Mountain
Bath
Wheelersfield
Hordley Cross
Quaw Hill
Holland Bay
Plantain Garden River
Goldon Grove
Old footpaths
Main Rd.
Secondry Rd
4WD Rd.
Footpath
Parish Boundary
Rivers
0 Kilometers 1 2 3 4 5
0 1 2 3
Miles

mountain cabbage (*Roystonea altissima*), found only in the east of Jamaica. On the ground may be the black, mulberry-like fruits of the bastard cedar (*Guazuma ulmifolia*).

The track once led to what was probably a coffee property. Bamboo-covered hillsides are an indication that the land was once cultivated. Look for the cart or carriage grooves in the limestone track leading to the ruined walls of a fortress-like structure, probably dating from the late eighteenth century. It was a time of slave revolts and rebellion, especially in this part of Jamaica, and it was not uncommon for a property house to be fortified.

ROWLANDSFIELD AND HAINING

Returning to the catchment, the track meets the road from the fording going east to Haining. It is best to walk this very picturesque road, as the limestone surface has deteriorated badly. It is crossed by several streams and bordered by trees, which encourage the thick growth of philodendrons, many varieties of ferns, pileas (*Urticaceae*) and *Piperaceae*. Varieties of all of these species are favourite pot plants abroad. There are the same tree species here as on the track to Big Level. You may be fortunate enough to see the Old Man Bird and other cuckoos in this area.

A scenic approach to this walk is from St. Thomas, taking the road from Hordley Cross to Rowlandsfield. The road climbs through limestone embankments of secondary forest, smallholdings and coconut groves. Several gardens along the way sport the attractive orange-flowered native shrub Fire Stick *Hamelia patens*. The forest walk is to the left at Haining. Ahead, the road goes down to the coast at Williamsfield, near Happy Grove school.

CHESTNUT BELLIED 'LIZARD' CUCKOO

FIRE STICK

REACH FALLS AND DRIVERS RIVER

REACH FALLS

Turning left along the coast road, after about 1 km (0.6 mi) a road turns inland to Reach, where there is a spectacular waterfall. It is worth visiting, if possible, for the richness of flora both upstream and downstream as well as the splendid falls and bathing pools.

ECCLESDOWN

BLAKEA URBANIANA

From Reach the road runs through Ecclesdown, passing a small bar on the way. Two long driveways are visible on the left, leading into the mountainside. The first is private property, but the second is an old forestry track that leads some 3 km (1.8 mi) into the mountainside until it is blocked by a rockfall and stream. There are many interesting trees and birds, and an uncommon climber, *Blakea urbaniana*, which is very similar to the Jamaican rose illustrated on page 17. The pink flower is slightly larger and flatter. It climbs over the roadside shrubs, drawing attention with its shiny green leaves that turn brilliant scarlet when they are about to fall.

Densely crowned nutmeg trees, 8 to 10 m (25 to 35 ft) high, grow in some gardens. You may see the yellow fruits, which split to show the brown nutmeg with surrounding red mace.

Guide to the Blue and John Crow Mountains

WEST INDIAN MAHOGANY

DOWN TREE (BALSA)

CAMBRIDGE BACKLANDS

About 8 km (5 mi) east along the coast road from Port Antonio, past the Blue Hole, is a turn inland at Fairy Hill to Sherwood Forest. It returns to Port Antonio, skirting the John Crow Mountains, and passes the Nonsuch Caves, which are privately owned and open to the public.

The nature lover should enjoy the Forestry Department road at Kenmay district, just beyond Sherwood Forest. It goes through Cambridge Backlands into the John Crow Mountains and is well worth a visit. By far the best way to enjoy this track, especially as there is a locked vehicle barrier at the entrance to the Forest Reserve, is to contact the Forestry Office at Folly, just East of Port Antonio (tel 876-993-3843). Mr Simpson is in charge. To those interested in knowing the forest, he is generous with his assistance. He seems to know every tree as he would know a personal friend. His energy and enthusiasm for his charges are infectious. If the forest warden, Mr Berry, a Maroon from Moore Town in the Rio Grande Valley, accompanies you, he will share his extensive knowledge of the medicinal uses of many of the plants. It is possible that guides could be assigned to

NUTMEG

MOSS AND LICHEN IN TREE

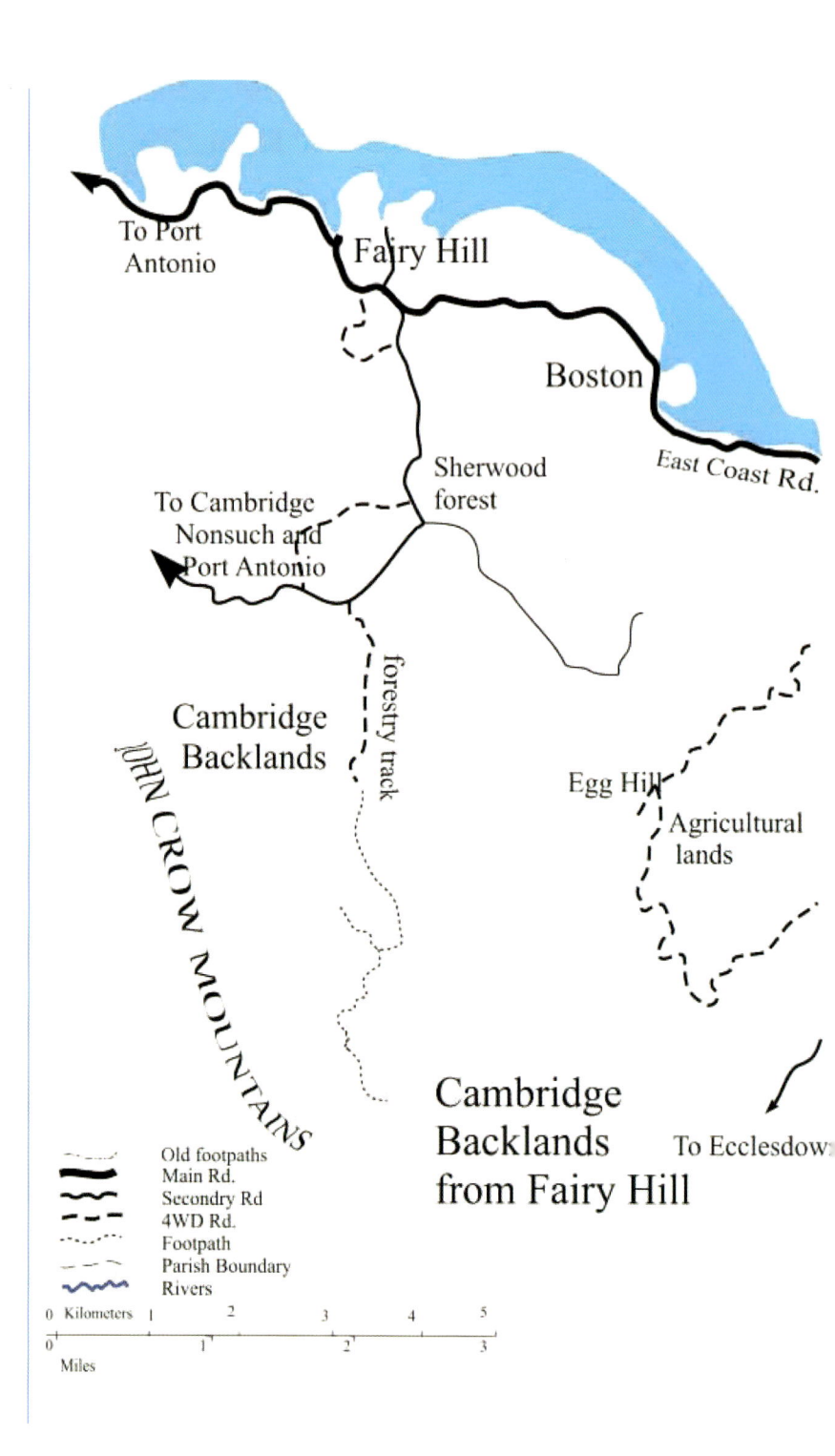

Cambridge Backlands from Fairy Hill

Map Legend:
- Old footpaths
- Main Rd.
- Secondry Rd
- 4WD Rd.
- Footpath
- Parish Boundary
- Rivers

Locations shown: To Port Antonio, Fairy Hill, Boston, East Coast Rd., Sherwood forest, To Cambridge Nonsuch and Port Antonio, Cambridge Backlands, forestry track, JOHN CROW MOUNTAINS, Egg Hill, Agricultural lands, To Ecclesdown

The Park and its Surroundings

this track in the future.

In planning this trip, remember that it rains most afternoons in Portland. Take along insect repellent, as the mosquitoes will swarm onto any exposed flesh, perhaps because the opportunity for human blood doesn't present itself very often. They are without guile, probably for the same reason – but while you are drawing satisfaction from disposing of six with one slap, another dozen are feasting off you elsewhere.

EPIPHYTIC FERNS

Approaching the settlement of Sherwood Forest, the first left turn goes to the school and the church. It is no longer a through road, although it used to return to the coast at Priestman's River, further east. Sherwood Forest is a pleasant community on a hill, overlooking a valley of tall forest trees, mainly Honduran mahogany. Some years ago, local farmers received saplings from the Forestry Department. The trees have matured, and the farmers have replanted and now earn an income by reaping and selling the lumber and by selling seeds from the trees back to the Forestry Department for propagation in its nurseries.

ORANGEQUIT

MARCGRAVIA SP

The next left turn takes you into the forest for several miles. The first mile of grassy road is through private property, which until a few years ago was a dairy farm but which, left to nature, has fairly quickly returned to forest. Among the trees are occasional patches of bananas and bamboo, and deeper into the forest some fruiting citrus and breadfruit trees have sprung up.

Growing thickly along this part of the track is a shrub known locally as bakra. It has shiny leaves and clusters of bright-pink berries, which turn black when ripe. Birds that feast on the berries easily propagate it.

At the barrier across the road a Forestry Department sign displays rules of the forest, which should be read and observed by anyone progressing further. Beyond this point the forest is maintained through protection, culling, replanting and natural

95

regeneration. Humid conditions facilitate growth, and the result is a rich and varied forest, composed of native and endemic species together with timber trees introduced from forestry nurseries. This is excellent for wildlife. Many birds live in the forest, as do bats, coneys and some wild hogs. Butterflies, other insects (including mosquitoes) and other invertebrates such as snails and hermit crabs are plentiful.

BROMELIADS

PHILODENDRON SPADIX AND SPATHE

STRANGLER FIG

EPIPHYTES

Most of the older trees carry a mass of epiphytes and parasites. There are several varieties of bromeliads perching on branches, some red, some green and others striped. There are clusters of orchids, some very small, and other plants such as the epiphytic *Columnea* with its dark, furry leaves and orange flowers. Decorating every tree and trailing through the undergrowth are two varieties of philodendron. These, like their relatives the wild cocos and anthuriums – also common here – have large leaves and very small flowers carried on a fleshy organ, the spadix, which is protected by the spathe. The hanging vines of the larger-leafed one are harvested and, when dry, are peeled and made into wicker furniture and baskets.

There are epiphytic and climbing ferns. At least 100 of the more than 600 ferns recorded in Jamaica have been found in this area, including the tree ferns and the ferns on the banks and in the undergrowth.

The strangler fig, or man jack, is an epiphyte that kills its host. It may grow from a seed lodged on the tree. As it grows, it puts down aerial roots and its branches surround and smother the foliage of the tree, killing it and taking its place. There is a huge cedar tree not far from the track at Bog Hill (so called because of the vehicles that have floundered, climbing it when it is wet). The cedar is enveloped in a strangler fig, and only a few branches of cedar foliage remain.

ROADSIDE PLANTS

BLAKEA

LANTANA

LOG WITH EPIDENDRUM ORCHID

Among the plants growing in and beside the road are several varieties of pilea, begonias and plants from the Melastomataceae family. Most striking is the *Blakea trinerva*, with waxy pink flowers up to 15 cm (6 ins) across, and elliptical green leaves that turn red when ready to drop. There are at least four varieties of gesnariad. One is the climbing *Columnea* already described under 'Epiphytes', above. Another, the red tube-flower, is seen growing in banks beside the road or on rocky ledges, grouped in rosettes of velvety leaves with central clusters of red or orange tubular flowers. The other two are known locally as 'search-me-heart'. They are taller. One has leaves up to 25 cm (10 in) long and grows to nearly 2 m (6 ft). The flowers are greenish-white and tubular. The slightly smaller one has small greenish-yellow flowers, spotted inside with purple-red. The leaves are boiled and used medicinally. Also medicinally used is pennyroyal, which grows in thick patches on the road. It smells strongly of peppermint when disturbed. There are occasional clumps of yellow-flowered heliconias, red-flowered pepper hibiscus, mauve-flowered and yellow-flowered sage or lantana and a white-flowered convolvulus with five-fingered leaves.

Sometimes the weight of epiphytes may bring down a branch of an old tree. On one such branch across the road, six varieties of orchid were found, mostly very small but two with the fragrant white flowers of the *Encyclia fragrans*. Three different bromeliads, one with a red flower, a *Peperomia*, a *Columnea*, ferns, lichens and part of the trailing philodendron were all on this one branch.

TREES

The trees in the forest range from small maiden plum trees (caution: all parts are poisonous) with a rosette of long leaves at the top, to very tall trees, such as greenheart and the silk cotton tree.

Tree ferns and palm trees are easily recognised. The most commonly seen palm is called 'thatch' here, but is known elsewhere as mountain cabbage palm. As its name implies, it is used as thatching material in this area. It has small red-purple fruits that are enjoyed by the White-crowned Pigeons.

Two other trees that you may see are called prickly yellow and yellow sanders; both have light-yellowish trunks, the first with conical spines up its trunk and branches, the second with spines only at the base.

The trumpet tree is common over the island in disturbed areas, growing up to 20 m (60 ft). It has large, lobed leaves with as many as 11 indentations, green on top and whitish underneath; fallen dried leaves are dark brown on top and whitish underneath. A common shrub in similar areas is woman wood, so called for the softness of its wood. Water mahoe, *Clusia flava* and the Santa Maria trees are described in chapter 4, on the John Crow Mountains flora.

Towering above these are tall timber trees, members of the sweetwood family, growing 20 to 25 m (65 to 80 ft) high; broadleaf, usually a very tall tree at 25 to 30

SANTA MARIA

TRUMPET TREE

GREENHEART

The Park and its Surroundings

GREEN HEART WOODY CAPSULES

GREEN HEART BASE

SILK COTTON

SILK COTTON TRUNK

m (80 to 100 ft), with incongruously small leaves; greenheart, as high as 30 m (100 ft); and several varieties of bulletwood. The wood from the greenheart and the bullets is hard, heavy and durable, formerly much used for construction and for railway sleepers. The silk cotton tree used to be far commoner than it is now. It is a giant of a tree, and was much prized and used to make seagoing dugout canoes for fishermen. Its main use now is for coffins. The tree grows to a height of 40 m (130 ft) and a girth of 12 m (40 ft); its branches spread out at right angles, and it has great buttress roots. The creamy white flowers come out before the five-fingered leaves, and three months after flowering, the seed capsules open and release the seeds, attached to white flossy kapok, which drifts to the ground. The kapok was used to stuff mattresses, life jackets and similar objects.

The tree was sacred to the Tainos, as the home of spirits. Until quite recently, tree cutters scattered a libation of rum around

SILK COTTON ON BRANCHES

99

the tree before felling it. One silk cotton tree grows near Bog Hill.

To augment the trees commonly found in this forest, the Forestry Department introduced seedlings from its nurseries, many of which are now mature. They include West Indian cedar, which has aromatic wood that repels insects, and panicles of greenish-white, fragrant flowers; mahoe, with yellow or red hibiscus-like flowers and hard, multicoloured wood; and Santa Maria, very tall and straight and found in damp areas. Its leaves are leathery, oblong and ribbed underneath.

MAHOGANY CAPSULE

There are also Jamaican mahogany trees, large and dense, with a large oval seed capsule packed with reddish-brown winged seeds. Its wood is preferred to the introduced Honduran mahogany, also growing here, which has larger leaves. Both are highly prized by cabinetmakers. There are young Spanish elm trees, which have fairly small leaves and bunches of sweet-smelling white flowers. The wood is tough and attractively shaded. There are a few perfume trees, also called ylang-ylang, a Magnoliaceae introduced from Asia. Its yellow flowers are very fragrant, and its seeds grow in a pink cluster.

RING TAILED PIGEON

Birds are plentiful in the forest, especially in the early morning, when the following maybe seen: Woodpeckers, Black-billed Streamertail hummingbirds, White-chinned Thrushes, White-crowned Pigeons (Bald Pate), Blue Pigeons or Crested Quail Doves (Mountain Witch), Zenaida Doves (Pea Dove),

The Park and its Surroundings

Becards, Jamaican Orioles, flocks of Yellow-billed Parrots and, occasionally, Black-billed Parrots, Parakeets and Ringtail Pigeons. High in several trees are large, untidy Becards' nests. In one tree there is a similar, but smaller, hanging nest of an Oriole.

Wild boars and rare coneys, which nest in hollowed-out, fallen tree stumps, are also known to inhabit this forest, as are Jamaican Giant Swallowtail butterflies (Pterourus homerus, formerly Papilio homerus).

THE RIO GRANDE VALLEY

RIO GRANDE LOOKING SOUTH

RIO GRANDE

The Rio Grande rises in the John Crow and easternmost Blue Mountains on the parish border separating St Thomas from Portland. Its many tributaries flow from the Blue Mountains and the John Crow Mountains to the east, and the majestic river flows north, to enter the sea near St. Margaret's Bay in Portland. The Rio Grande Valley is known for its exceptionally high

RIO GRANDE VALLEY FROM MOUNTAINS

annual precipitation. It is acknowledged to be one of the wettest places on earth. For 1 m (39 in) or more of rain to fall in a month is not unusual. As a result, landslides are frequent during heavy rains, and the river often changes course due to silting and erosion of its banks. In such conditions, road maintenance is difficult.

RAFTING

RIO GRANDE RAFTING

The Rio Grande is famous for the bamboo rafts on which farmers once poled their bananas and other produce downriver. Nowadays, rafting the river is a pleasure trip. Enquire at Rafter's Rest, tel 876-993-5778. The cost per raft and for your vehicle to be driven from the boarding place to Rafter's Rest should be agreed upon ahead of time. Berridale is the boarding point, from which you'll be poled leisurely downstream on a bamboo raft, through a tranquil tropical landscape to Rafter's Rest, where the Rio Grande enters the sea. There is often interesting bird life along the way, and the rafters will stop for picnicking and swimming. Berridale is accessible from picturesque Port

The Park and its Surroundings

CHRIST CHURCH PORT ANTONIO

PORT ANTONIO TOWN HALL

Antonio, capital of Portland, which in the 1930s was a bustling banana exporting port. There are still some handsome historic buildings, such as the courthouse and De Montevin Lodge.

The road to Berridale and the Rio Grande Valley goes inland beside Port Antonio's

NEAR BERRIDALE

103

LOCAL NAMES OF PLANTS IN TEXT AND BOTANICAL NAMES OR FAMILIES

Columnea	*Columnea hirsuta*
Red tube-flower	*Gesneria acaulis*
Penny royal	*Satureja brownei*
Yellow sage, purple sage	*Lantana* spp.
Search-me-heart	*Rytidophyllum tomentosum*
Maiden plum	*Comocladia pinnatifolia*
Greenheart, Break-axe tree, Ironwood	*Sloanea jamaicensis*
Silk cotton	*Ceiba pentandra*
Thatch/Mountain cabbage palm	*Roystonea altissima*
Prickly yellow	*Fagara martinicensis*
Yellow sanders	*Fagara flava*
Trumpet tree	*Cecropia peltata*
Sweetwoods	*Lauraceae* family
Broadleaf	*Terminalia latifolia*
Bullets	*Sapotaceae* family
Water mahoe	*Hernandia catalpifolia*
West Indian mahogany	*Swietenia mahogoni*
Honduran mahogany	*Swietenia macrophylla*
Santa Maria	*Callophyllum calaba*
Spanish elm	*Cordia gerascanthus*
West Indian cedar	*Cedrela odorata*
Blue mahoe	*Hibiscus elatus*

The Park and its Surroundings

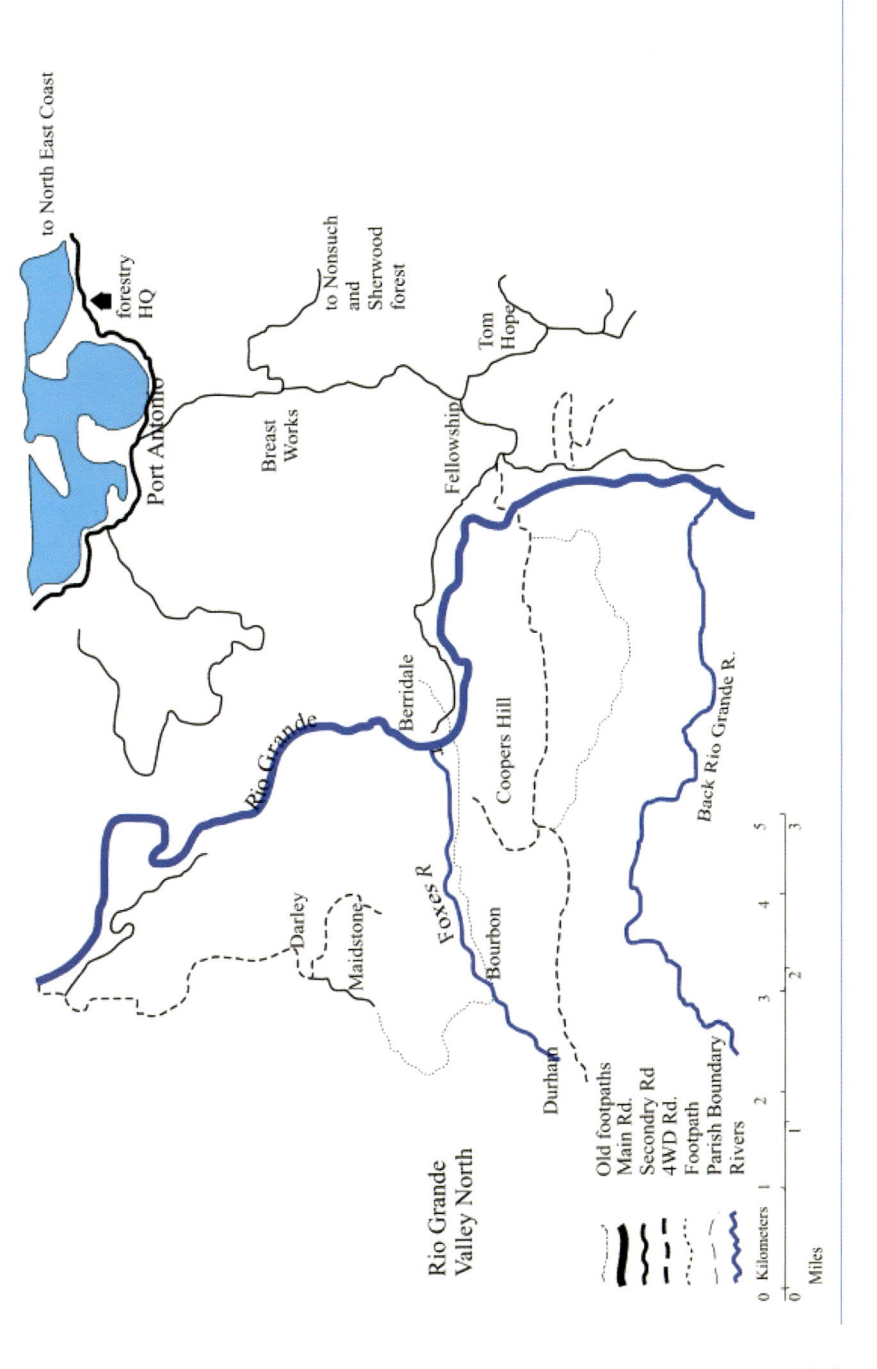

TITCHFIELD PENINSULAR PORT ANTONIO

attractive Anglican church. It passes through Breastworks to the intersection at Fellowship, a distance of 6 km (3.75 mi). The right fork leads to Berridale, where the Rio Grande is joined by Foxes River.

RIVERSIDE TRAILS

There are three footpaths on the west side of the Rio Grande. They go to the communities of Cooper's Hill, Durham and Samba Hill, with the Back Rio Grande to the left. The picturesque path beside Foxes River has the added attraction of a cave and the Scatter waterfalls. At Burbon, a distance of 5.6 km (3.5 mi), a path bears left to Durham and right to Maidstone, from where a 8 km (5 mi) rough road goes to the bridge at St Margaret's Bay. Another path from Berridale follows the Rio Grande and then meets the previously mentioned track to St. Margaret's Bay. There is also a trail from Berridale that meets the road between Breastworks and Fellowship.

THE MAROON SETTLEMENTS

At Fellowship, bear left to continue up the Rio Grande Valley. Windsor, 5.6 km (3.5 mi) away, on Dons River, is the next community of any size. A road to the right leads to several

The Park and its Surroundings

MILLBANK FARMER

hiking trails on the far side of the Rio Grande, and there is another trail to the left. Ahead the road continues to Seaman's Valley, where the remains of fortifications indicate that this was the site of a battle between Maroons and British sailors, who may have pursued the runaway slaves to this point. However, a steep hill nearby, commanding a broad view, was undoubtedly a lookout point from which to 'see man'. Hidden in vegetation, a waterfall cascades down a rock face not far above the road.

MOORE TOWN

MOORE TOWN

WILD PIG

Ahead on the main road are the autonomous Maroon communities of Moore Town and Cornwall Barracks. Moore Town is the centre of Maroon culture in the Rio Grande Valley. There is a monument to National Hero Nanny of the Maroons, who is buried here. She successfully led the rebellious Maroons against the British soldiers and sailors. A nearby waterfall is named after her. A museum was opened in 1995.

107

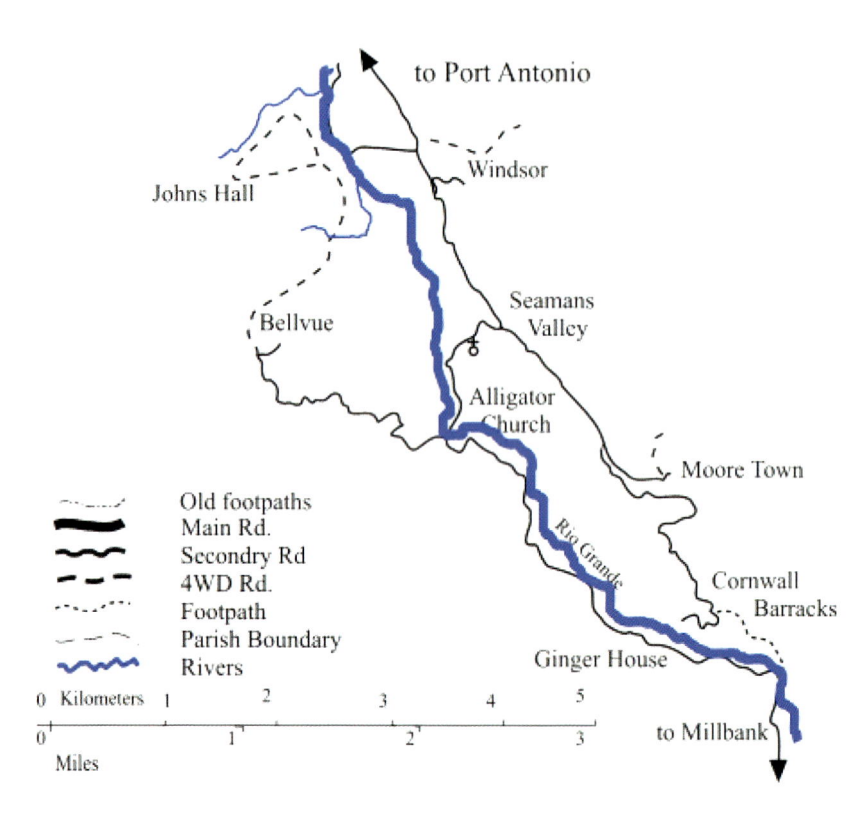

Maroon Settlements
in Rio Grande Valley

© JEREMY FRANCIS

JOHN CROW MOUNTAINS

GINGER HOUSE BRIDGE

GINGER LILY

Cornwall Barracks, as its name implies, was a British barrack. Here, beside Jupiter Falls, are a cave and a mineral spring. Sister Ivy operates a bathhouse specialising in aromatic oils. She also runs a craft centre that demonstrates the uses of traditional plant material from the forest. It is only a short walk to Ginger House on the road, which forks right at Seaman's Valley going towards Millbank and Bowden Pen, the farthest point into the valley that is accessible by vehicle.

MILLBANK AND BOWDEN PEN

Continuing along the road, 2.4 km (1.5 mi) to the right of Seaman's Valley is the bridge at Alligator Church, a structure that reveals its age when seen from beneath. The road and the many bridges of the Rio Grande Valley were constructed in the late 1920s and early 1930s,

GIANT SWALLOWTAIL

to facilitate the transport of bananas for shipment from Port Antonio. The dates can be seen under some of the bridges. Many of them are of the type of construction used for railways. Sugar had been tried in the valley in earlier days, but the climate proved too wet. Coffee superseded the pine trees planted on the higher slopes after they were felled by hurricane Gilbert in 1988. Dasheen, a root vegetable, is now a major crop. Its relatives, the variegated Caladiums and wild cocos (Araceae granifolium), along with wild ginger (Hedychium), grow thickly on the bank sides and up into the hills all along the valley. Their tuberous roots form a dense mat, which prevents soil erosion. Between Ginger House and Comfort Castle there is a trail to the

Guide to the Blue and John Crow Mountains

left from Cornwall Barracks; the two trails to the right meet and follow the Dry River, a tributary of the Rio Grande.

Millbank, where one year the highest rainfall in the world was recorded, is surrounded by streams bouncing over rocks. Along these streams where the water mahoe grows, it is possible to glimpse the Jamaican Giant Swallowtail butterfly (*Pterourus homerus*, formerly *Papilio homerus*) flitting through the foliage, as the water mahoe is its food plant.

WHITE RIVER FALLS: THERE AND BACK

The White River Falls are reached by a narrow suspension bridge over the Rio Grande near Millbank. The bridge was a project of the Jamaica Conservation and Development Trust (JCDT). This organisation manages the Blue and John Crow Mountains National Park. If it is dry enough (and remember, it rains nearly all year round in the valley), it can be a round trip, as one approaches the falls along the White River, clambering over rocks and wading through the water. Before reaching the riverbed the path is narrow, running between waist-high ferns and ginger lilies. The other route is via an uphill path followed by a steep descent. At one point the falls can be seen ahead through thick foliage. Look for the climbing bamboo and a climbing orange-flowered Gesneria.

BRIDGE AT MILLBANK

CASCADE

The local community welcomes visitors. There is a Maroon celebration each New Year. Homes offering B&B and camping are available in the area, but most of them are not registered with the Jamaica Tourist Board. The same applies to many of the attractions. The visitor should get advice in Port Antonio from the Tourist

111

SECOND FALL WHITE RIVER © E. GARRAWAY

Board (tel 876-993-3051, 876-993-2587 or 876-993-4150) at City Centre Plaza, or from Valley Hikes (876-993-3881), 12 West Street. In Kingston, contact Joy Douglas at 876-929-8824 for Valley Hikes, which arranges guided hiking on the trails described here and others. There is a charge for guiding services, including transport to and from Port Antonio (see appendix). From a guide you will learn local names of fauna and flora, medicinal and culinary uses of plants and their uses in Maroon culture. Another tour company is Sunventure Tours, tel 876-960-6685.

BOWDEN PEN AND MAROON CULTURE

Ask for Linette Wilks, a Maroon from Bowden Pen, and enquire about guides and transport. She is a dynamic woman whose enthusiasm for the culture and history of the Maroons is infectious. She has comfortable, rustic cabins at Bowden Pen, the end of the road before climbing the Cuna Cuna Pass to Bath towards Corn Puss Gap and into St. Thomas (see the section 'Bath and the Mountains') This is a true back-to-nature experience in a mystical, charming setting, often enveloped by mist. You will need flashlights and rain gear. Experience valley bush cooking – green bananas, a variety of tubers, Bussu (a tiny water snail used to make a tasty soup), janga (crayfish) and wild boar. The Maroons originated jerk pork, now available throughout Jamaica.

THE NORTHERN SECTION

The Grand Ridge of the Blue Mountains runs nearer to the south coast than to the north coast of Jamaica, and the northern slopes receive more rainfall and are more thickly wooded. Access is therefore more difficult.

Nevertheless, before motor transport there were well-used trails connecting north and south, along which people traveled with mules, donkeys and horses to carry their produce. One

The Park and its Surroundings

FERNY BANK

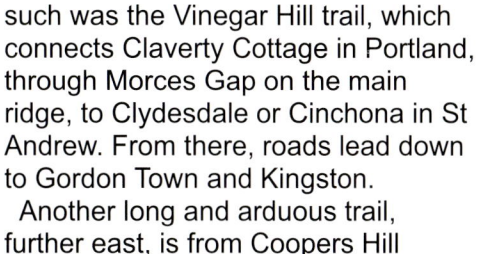

such was the Vinegar Hill trail, which connects Claverty Cottage in Portland, through Morces Gap on the main ridge, to Clydesdale or Cinchona in St Andrew. From there, roads lead down to Gordon Town and Kingston.

Another long and arduous trail, further east, is from Coopers Hill (Portland), or from Windsor in the Rio Grande Valley, to the site of Nanny Town. Nanny Town was the headquarters of the Eastern Maroons, led by Nanny and Quaco, or Quao, in the early eighteenth century. There is little to see, as Nanny Town was thoroughly destroyed by the British army. By that time, however, Nanny had withdrawn her people, and the war continued (see chapter 2, 'The Historical Background'). An expedition, transported by helicopter, excavated the site in the 1990s, but little was found. It was established that Maroons and Tainos, who first used it as a hideout, had cohabited there. Both the Vinegar Hill and Nanny Town trails require expert guides, adequate food and water and camping gear. See appendix for sources of information, tour guides, and so forth.

An idea of the terrain can be gained by travelling down the Buff Bay road, and by travelling along the small roads (4WD recommended) which run through the river valleys, connecting settlements south of the north coast road.

THE BUFF BAY ROAD

This is a good road that accompanies the Buff Bay River from the mountains to the sea. It suffered landslides from hurricane damage in 2005. It begins at Section, between Holywell and Silver Hill Gap, and at first it runs through an old forestry plantation. The tall mahoe trees have brilliant yellow flowers instead of the usual dark red. The river runs along the valley to the east until it reaches Silver Hill, where a bridge

113

CASCADE FALLS

crosses over it. The west bank of the upper part of the road is steep hillside and rock, broken by waterfalls tumbling down to the river below. On rocky ledges there are clumps of the Jamaican Pitcairnia, a bromeliad species with long, narrow, prickly green leaves and, in spring, tall red flowers. There are a number of footpaths, both on the right side, down to the river valley, and to the left, running uphill. Some of these lead to properties, but the paths that used to continue past the houses to Hardwar Gap or Holywell are now mostly disused.

The road passes through Cascade – noted for its waterfalls – and then Cedar Valley and Wakefield. There are many small settlements on the way down to Buff Bay. Charles Town was originally a settlement granted to the Maroons after the 1739 agreement with the British to cease hostilities (see chapter 2).

A Maroon museum has been built here, next to the ritual ground (Asufa) where traditional Maroon ceremonies and dancing are still held. To visit the museum ask for Miss Kim or contact Frank Lumsden (tel 876-445-2861). High up above Charles Town on the west side of the valley is the site of an early Maroon village, Crawford Town, which has yet to be fully investigated. On the west side, across the Buff Bay River

ASUFA

Guide to the Blue and John Crow Mountains

The Park and its Surroundings

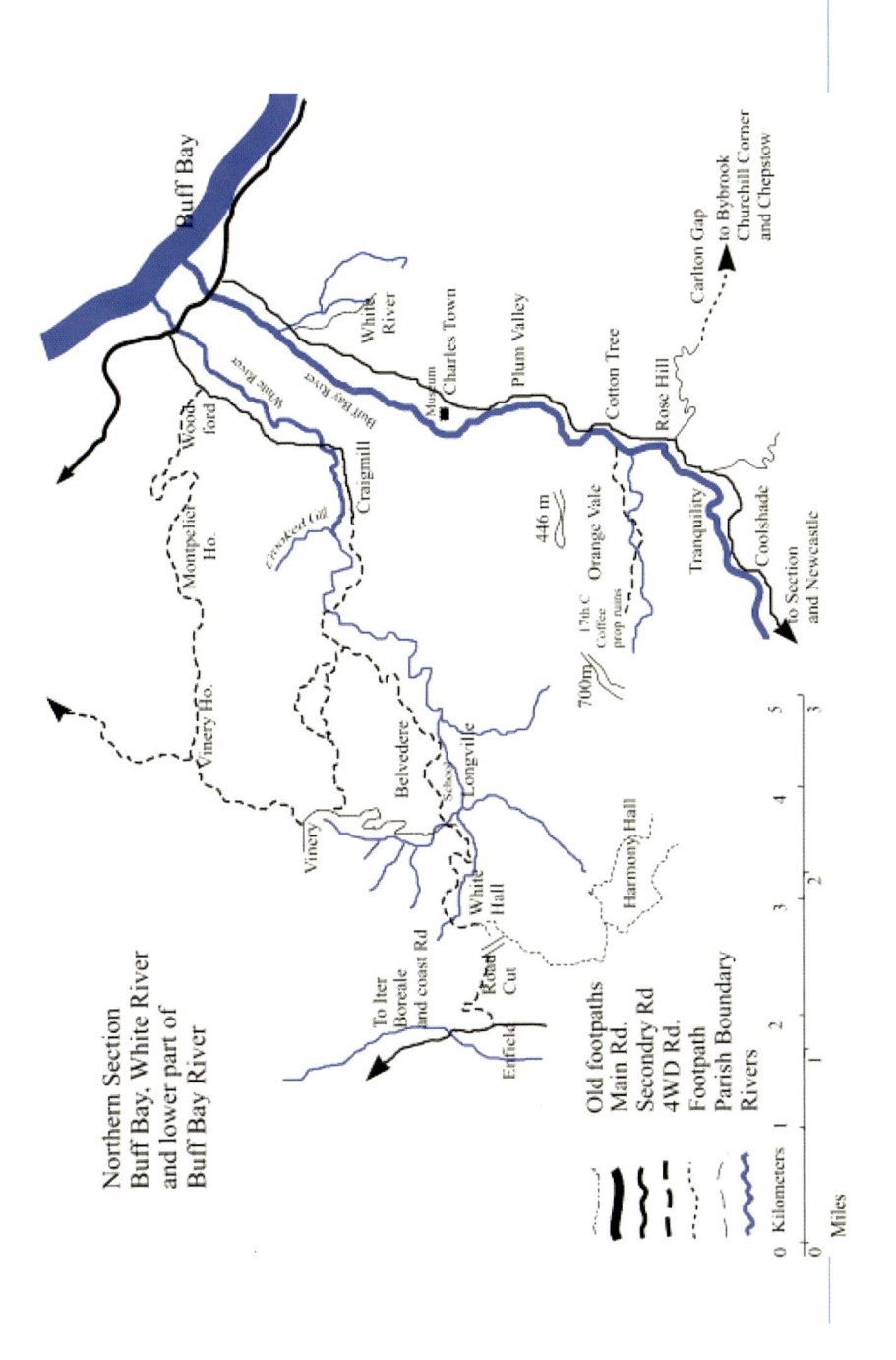

Northern Section
Buff Bay, White River and lower part of Buff Bay River

CYCLISTS' HALT
© JILL BYLES

from the small settlement of Cotton Tree, a steep track leads up a wooded hillside to the extensive ruins of an eighteenth-century coffee plantation. Among the tall trees can be found the stone walls of the slave quarters and possibly a hospital, numerous barbecues for drying the coffee, the site of a water wheel and an aqueduct leading to it. Water must have been channelled to it from the river seen streaming down from the hill above. For further information on the Maroons and the Charles Town area, contact Keith or Frank Lumsden, tel 876-445-2861. Buff Bay is a bustling country town. Blue Mountain Bicycle Tours Ltd (tel 876-974-7075) runs a popular downhill trip from here, taking a busload of cyclists and another load of bicycles to Hardwar Gap, by Holywell, from where the party cycles to Section and then down the road to Buff Bay.

They stop at Silver Hill for lunch and swimming in the waterfall nearby the first of two Fish Dunn falls in the neighbourhood.

FISH DUNN FALLS
© S. HODGES

West from Buff Bay there are two bridges, the first over the Buff Bay River and, soon after, one over the White River, where a track turns inland. There are several White Rivers in Jamaica, named for the striking white limestone riverbeds. This one winds through small plantations of coconuts, pastureland and small settlements. The track crosses some old bridges and gets very rough. It stops on a ridge named Whitehall. Formerly it ran down into the next valley and rejoined the coastal road, but it has been destroyed by flooding. A footpath into the now disused forestry reserve above Whitehall gives glimpses of the valley and is a good place to

JAMAICA TALL COCONUTS

see birds. There are bathing pools downriver from the bridge at Craigmill. If exploring the Buff Bay area on foot, you can find reasonable accommodation at Blueberry Hill Guest House, Kildare (tel 876-913-6814), overlooking the sea just east of Buff Bay, on a road adjoining the Buff Bay road, or at Rivers Edge near Annotto Bay (see appendix).

SPANISH RIVER

NATURES PLACE

The Spanish River runs into the sea between Buff Bay and Orange Bay. As you approach the river mouth you will see the sign 'Nature's Place'. This is a well-kept property extending to the river mouth and sea, with a waterway and a boat that can be rented. Tents can be rented or you can pitch your own, and there is plenty of room for privacy on the extensive lawns and in the guava orchard. Toilet facilities are provided, and organic meals are available. Contact Mr F. White, tel 876-926-6765.

Turning east from Buff Bay some 4 km 2 ½ miles, brings you to an oblique road running inland. It passes through magnificent trees with hanging vines to reach the Spanish river.

COFFEE AT SHIRLEY CASTLE

The Park and its Surroundings

It continues to Chepstow where the road ahead climbs until it reaches Claverty Cottage. It must be the very worst "main road" in Jamaica. A lot of coffee is grown in the area, and a better track from a coffee factory in the valley to the left joins the road about two-thirds of the way up. This links with the road to Shirley Castle and the Swift river which returns to the coast road at Hope Bay. From Claverty Cottage you look straight across the valley where the Vinegar Hill trail formerly ran, to the Grand ridge of the Blue Mountains, John Crow peak to the west, Sir John's ahead, High Peak east. Blue Mountain peak is less visible, further southeast. Mist swirls around the peaks most days to add to the scene.

FISH DUNN FALLS (2)

WHITE RIVER

Soon after leaving Chepstow on the road to Claverty Cottage, after passing a sports ground, the road bends and begins to rise. An old parochial road on the left, now grassy, leads to private property on the right, with a footpath leading left and down to the steep bank of the river gorge. Water from the mountains tumbles over huge rocks, a spectacular sight which changes as you climb. At one

MOUNTAINS FROM CLAVERTY COTTAGE

119

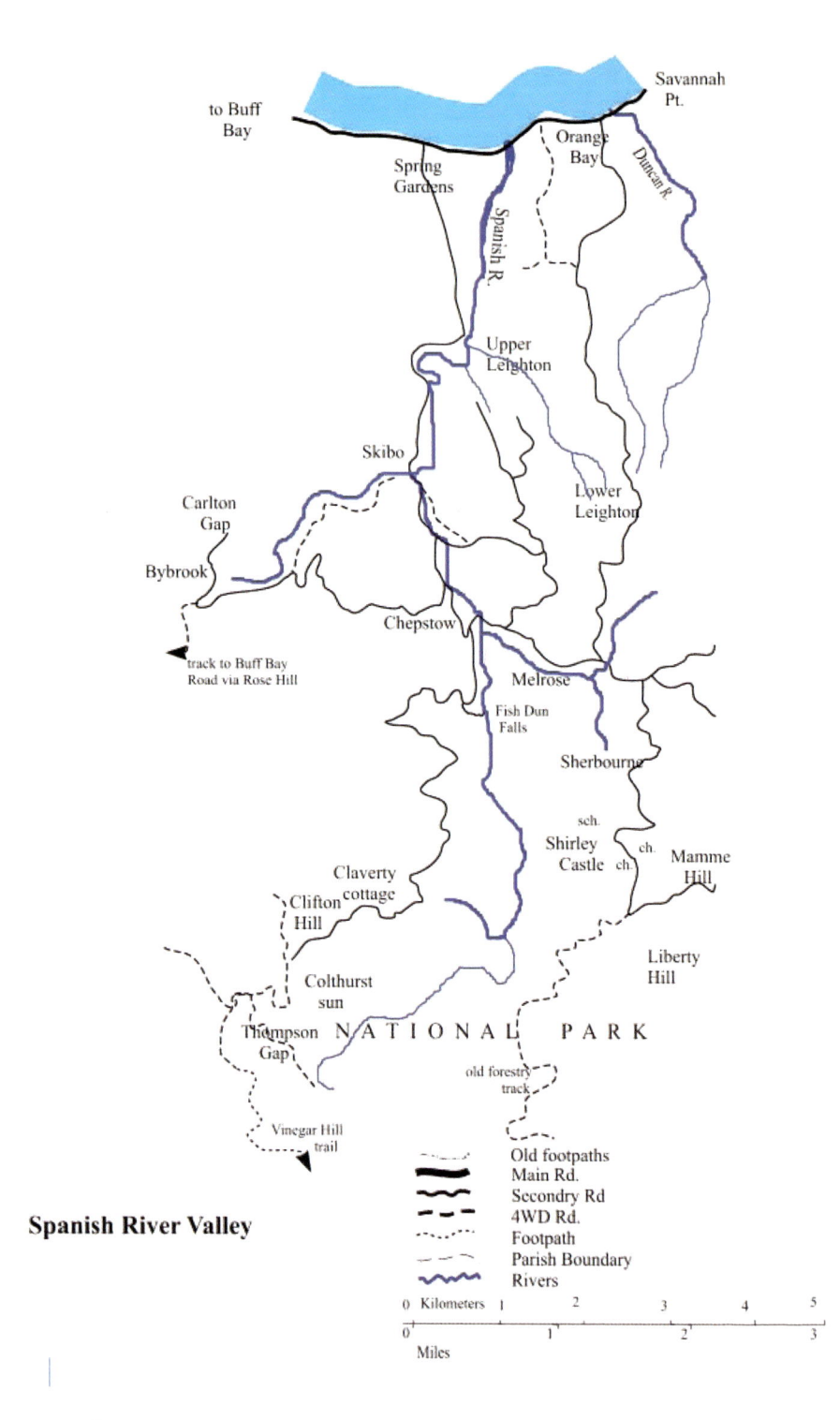

Spanish River Valley

The Park and its Surroundings

RED TUBE GESNERIA

CACOON POD

point steps lead down (and up, further on), and it is possible to clamber down and bathe in the lowest pool.

On the upper side of the path there is lush vegetation – particularly ferns, mosses and the red tube-flower (Gesnaria acaulis) – clustering in the rock crevices. Interesting fungi grow along the path, and large beans lie scattered on the ground from the overhead cacoon vine (Entada gigas), which spreads among the trees. The huge pods may be more than a metre long and contain 10 or so beans. The Dutchman's pipe pictured is an insectivorous plant.

THE FORESTRY ROAD

There is a network of small roads between the Spanish and Swift rivers and their tributaries. From Chepstow on the Spanish River, from Orange Bay and Hope Bay, roads meander south. The road through Shirley Castle or through Mammee Hill comes to a high point where an old forestry road bears south into a valley six or seven kilometers inside the park boundary. The road runs into the forestry reserve not far from its end. A new road forks right, into a steep valley where a coffee factory has been built and continues to meet the road

CALICO FLOWER OR
DUTCHMAN'S PIPE

to Claverty Cottage. Most of the hill slopes around have been taken over for coffee. Unfortunately, many areas have been clear-cut and herbicides have been applied, so bare earth surrounds the bushes. Some areas seem to have been abandoned, and trumpet trees, a sign of disturbance, struggle up under a network of vines. Other sections, including the road banks and further ridges, have pines planted by the Forestry Department and many indigenous trees and shrubs. There are many clumps of tree ferns and other ferns, and pink and white begonias line the roadside in some sections.

SPATHODIA

Guide to the Blue and John Crow Mountains

The Park and its Surroundings

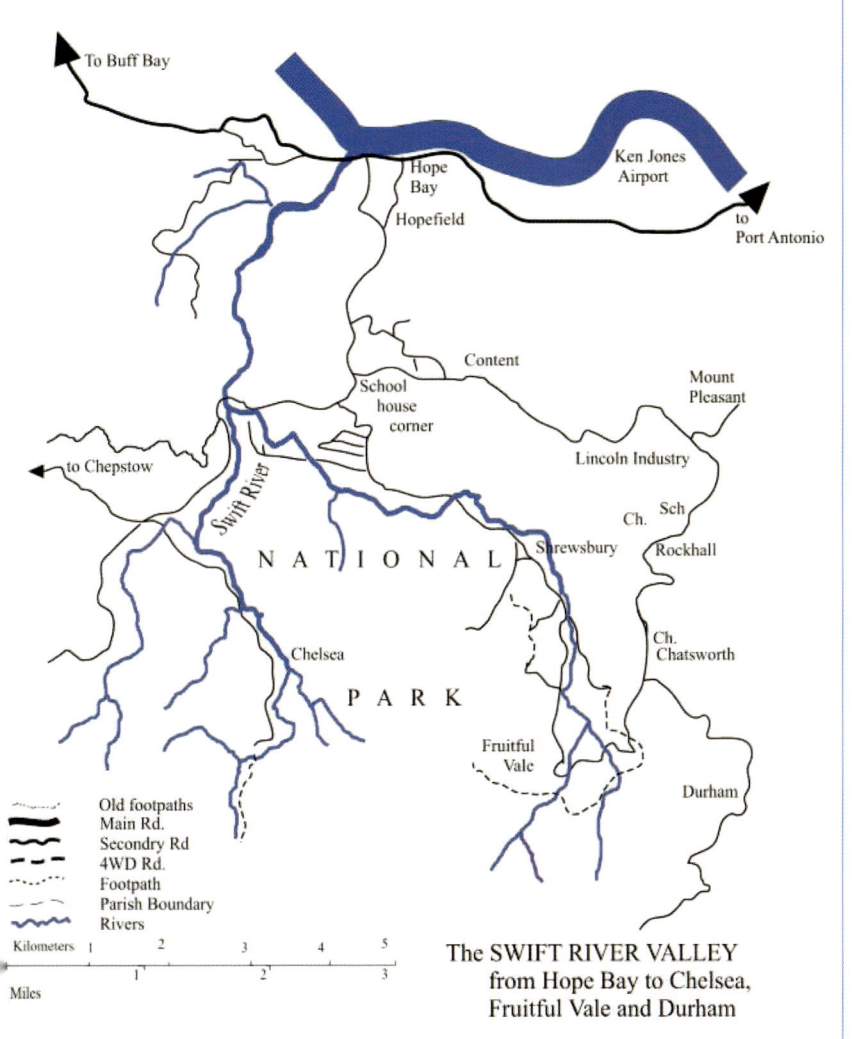

The SWIFT RIVER VALLEY from Hope Bay to Chelsea, Fruitful Vale and Durham

123

CHELSEA

RED CONE FLOWER

THE SWIFT RIVER

The road inland from Hope Bay leads to the junction of the Swift River and the Back River from Fruitful Vale, a flourishing agricultural village. Following the river southward, you come to Bloomfields and then Chelsea. Chelsea is a pleasant village on the riverside. Ramps and steps have been built down to the river, where there are unspoiled pools and small beaches for bathing and exploring. Shaded resting spots have been built above, and a suspension footbridge crosses the river.

At the very end of the village, a trail runs into the forest, following the river. The trees make it cool and dark, but the darkness is punctuated by brightly flowering red cone plants (*Pachystrachis coccinea*), which grow freely along the path and river.

Further trails are described in the section on the Rio Grande Valley (pp. 101–103).

SWIFT RIVER NEAR CHELSEA

Guide to the Blue and John Crow Mountains

THE HISTORICAL BACKGROUND

Mary Langford

THE TAINOS

TAINO ARTIFACTS

    The earliest inhabitants of Jamaica were the Arawak-speaking Indians, the Tainos. They settled on low hills not far from the sea, 'within reach of a good canoe beach'. Their staple diet was cassava and fish. The women cultivated edible plants, and the men brought in fish and game. Later some spread inland. However, in 1494 Columbus and the Spanish 'discovered' Jamaica, and in 1509 an expedition was sent from Spain to colonise the island. The Tainos were enslaved and forced to work for the settlers under very harsh conditions. They resisted, and many died, committed suicide or fled to the mountains, where they eked out an existence in small settlements.

THE MAROONS

The Spanish then brought in slaves from Spain, some probably Moors, others West Africans from the Portuguese slave trade. Some escaped to the mountains and eventually joined the Tainos. They were called cimarron, meaning 'wild and untamed', by the Spanish, from which the British probably derived the word 'maroon'.

When the British attacked the island in 1655, the Spanish governor freed the slaves in the hope that they might help defend the island. By 1658, however, the British had secured a firm footing, and the Spanish retreated to Hispaniola. The

NORTHERN SLOPES

Maroons and freed slaves remained as free people in the mountains. More slaves were brought in by the British from Africa, and some escaped to join the Maroons, who frequently harassed the settlers for supplies.

The Maroons who roamed the northern slopes of the Blue Mountains became skilful guerilla fighters, living by hunting wild hogs brought in by the Spanish, planting small patches of ground provisions (yams, eddoes and plantains), and raiding the English settlers. They would set fire to outlying estates and steal provisions, including livestock and machetes and guns.

Their small settlements could be moved quickly when necessary. For a while Nanny Town, to the northeast of Blue Mountain Peak, was a Maroon headquarters in the east under the leadership of Quao (or Quaco) and Nanny. The Maroons

The Historical Background

communicated in African dialects, Spanish and English and used the abeng, or cow horn, to send messages over long distances.

The parish of Portland was established in 1723, by order of the then governor of Jamaica, the Duke of Portland. But in spite of generous inducements, the settlers could not survive the depredations of the Maroons.

After years of failure to exterminate or even subdue the Maroons, the British signed a 'stand-off' peace in 1739 with Cudjoe in the west, and later with Quao (or Quaco) in the east, whereby lands were granted to the Maroons, hostilities ceased and the Maroons would no longer harbour runaway slaves. Settlements in the Rio Grande Valley, such as Seaman's Valley, Moore Town and Cornwall Barracks, and Charlestown in the Buff Bay Valley, were all developed by Maroon descendants who remained in the east and are well-known to most Portlanders. Quaw Hill in St. Thomas and Quaco Falls, near the Cuna Cuna Pass, are named after Quao/Quaco.

COFFEE

As early as 1728 the then governor, Sir Nicholas Lawes, had introduced coffee into his own estate in the Blue Mountain foothills and found it did well in the soil and climate.

During the revolution in Haiti (then St. Dominque) in 1792, several coffee planters fled to Jamaica, where they acquired land in the Blue Mountains and successfully grew coffee. At the same time, because of declining profits in sugar, some Jamaican planters also acquired land in the mountains and set

WALLENFORD COFFEE FACTORY

COFFEE FIELD

up coffee estates. It would have been a common sight to see slaves planting and pruning, picking and carrying cherry-ripe beans to be processed and, later, carrying the clean green beans to Kingston to be exported.

Most estates had their own pulperies, barbecues and property marks. The best known were Abbey Green, Moy Hall, Radnor, Silverhill and Wallenford. Coffee grown on these estates was known as Blue Mountain coffee and was considered superior, fetching good prices in England.

After the abolition of slavery in 1838, former slaves were able to acquire land to cultivate crops of their own choice. Many moved into the mountains to cultivate coffee, ground provisions and flowers for the market.

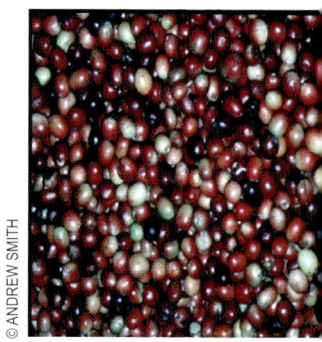

COFFEE BEANS

The big estate owners found it difficult to produce profitably, with scarce labour and competition from Brazil, which was flooding the market in the 1840s. Coffee became profitable again in the 1880s, at which time Mr Cecil Munn bought Strawberry Hill, near Cinchona, to plant and process coffee. His son, Victor, started the Mavis Bank Central Coffee Factory, where cherry-ripe coffee is still processed.

NEWCASTLE

In 1841 Sir William Gomm, KCB, commander of the British forces in Jamaica, persuaded the authorities to purchase the old coffee properties of Newcastle and Middleton to construct a permanent hill-station 1,220 m (4,000 ft) above the fever-prone plains. The previous loss of life from yellow fever and malaria for soldiers fresh to the tropics had been appalling. This changed significantly after Newcastle was opened. The camp continued to house British troops until Jamaica became independent in 1962, when it was converted to a training station for the Jamaica Defence Force.

PRINT FROM NEWCASTLE MESS

KINGSTON FROM NEWCASTLE

129

THE MORANT BAY REBELLION

After emancipation in 1838 and the end of the apprenticeship period in 1840, there was a movement away from the estates by former slaves. Many were assisted by their churches and the Baptist Free Village scheme to rent or purchase land for cultivation and to build a home. Others took up work – for example, as carpenters, masons and fishermen.

This left the planters with insufficient workers to operate their plantations. Some sold up and left, but others carried on. Still holding legislative and judicial power, they passed innumerable laws over the next 25 years to try to reverse the trend and to prevent access to the legislature of those trusted by the peasantry.

Land was made difficult to acquire, and taxes were imposed on basic items such as food, clothes, small carts and donkeys. As conditions worsened, crime increased – and was met by savage punishment.

In the 1850s and 1860s, conditions became critical. Droughts were followed by crop failures; smallpox and cholera spread, killing 32,000 people in 1850–51; cheap imports, grain and salt fish became scarce during the American Civil War.

Petitions to Queen Victoria and Governor Eyre for land to be made available for cultivation and for relief from onerous taxes elicited no response.

Things came to a head in 1865. Paul Bogle, a farmer and Baptist deacon in Stony Gut, gained a large following, and when petitions to the governor and the custos (senior magistrate) of St. Thomas were ignored, he took on the custos, a large landowner and president of the magistrates' court. Bogle and his supporters attended the court in Morant Bay, challenging verdicts they thought unfair and harassing the magistrates. Bogle and his followers were summoned to attend court, charged with obstruction, on October 11, and an angry crowd accompanied the accused to the court-house. The custos had prepared for trouble by installing military forces at the court. He immediately read the Riot Act,

PAUL BOGLE © S. HODGES

The Historical Background

CINCHONA (BUILT AROUND 1876)

and the militia fired into the crowd. Mayhem followed, with the court officials fleeing and the crowd setting fire to the schoolhouse and opening the prison.

Martial law was proclaimed, and after a week of fighting, Bogle was captured by the Maroons and handed over at Morant Bay. The next day he was court-martialled and hanged. Reprisals were savage: beatings followed by hanging. Some 1,000 homes were burnt and crops destroyed. The loss of life was estimated at over 1,000.

When Governor Eyre was recalled to Britain to report, he had a cold reception. Jamaica was made a Crown Colony, and Sir John Peter Grant was sent as governor. He instituted reforms to improve the lot of the many who had been so poorly treated, and brought about some economic stability.

FORESTRY

BELLEVUE (BUILT EARLY 20TH CENTURY)

By the end of the nineteenth century and the beginning of the twentieth, it was becoming obvious that excessive deforestation and cultivation on the steep slopes was leading to soil erosion and degradation of watersheds, and that the government must act. It was not until 1937, however, that a comprehensive forest law was passed and a viable Forestry Department set up. Clydesdale, a former coffee property, was acquired as a tree nursery. Many species were grown, including blue mahoe, eucalyptus, juniper cedar and silky oak, though in the 1960s the emphasis was on Caribbean pine. Unfortunately, the pine did not stand up to hurricane Gilbert in 1988, and the Forestry Department lost heavily.

MARKET CROPS

In the 1950s, the government made efforts to encourage terracing by small farmers, in order to control erosion when they grew thyme, escallion, carrots and flowers. The Coffee Marketing Board was set up to assist in re-establishing small-scale coffee growing.

TOURISM

Tourism began in a small way, with visitors and local people exploring the mountains, especially climbing the Blue Mountain Peak. Whitfield Hall was opened to travellers in 1925, and in

VIEW FROM FLAMSTEAD

1937 Miss Steadman opened a guesthouse, Torre Garda, at Penlyne Castle. Other early holiday venues were at Pine Grove, near Guava Ridge, and at Flamstead. Pine Grove was popular in the 1940s for cool holidays, and also for picnics and weddings. It is now a children's home. The Forestry Department allowed the use of its accommodation at Clydesdale, Holywell, Portland Gap and the Peak, and others soon followed. In 1992 the National Park, with its 80,000 hectares (200,000 acres) of land, became a reality – for conservation of the island's largest watershed, for biodiversity, and for the recreation and enjoyment of Jamaicans and visitors alike.

WHITEFIELD HALL (BUILT MID 18TH CENTURY)

FURTHER READING

Clinton Black *History of Jamaica* (London: Collins Educational). Black was the government archivist in Kingston. This concise book, covering the period from the Tainos to independence, is the classic introduction to Jamaica's history.

Beverley Carey *The Maroon Story*. The Authentic and Original History of the Maroons in the History of Jamaica 1490-1880 (St Andrew: Agouti Press). The story of escaped slaves in Jamaica and the autonomous and rebellious communities they formed during the colonial period.

Philip Sherlock and Hazel Bennett *The Story of the Jamaican People* (Kingston: Ian Randle Publishers). The history of the Jamaican people from an Afro-Jamaican rather than a European perspective.

THE GEOLOGY

Ryan Ramsook

THE BLUE MOUNTAINS

The Blue Mountain Range contains the largest area 600 km2 (375 mi2) of Cretaceous (older than 65 million years) rocks in Jamaica, which are known as the Blue Mountain Inlier (see Figure 1). The inlier contains an array of sedimentary, igneous and metamorphic rocks of early to late Cretaceous age (140 to 65 million years old). De La Beche (1827), the first person to survey the rocks of the Blue Mountains, produced the first geological map of eastern Jamaica, arguably the oldest geological map in the Western Hemisphere.

The unique geology

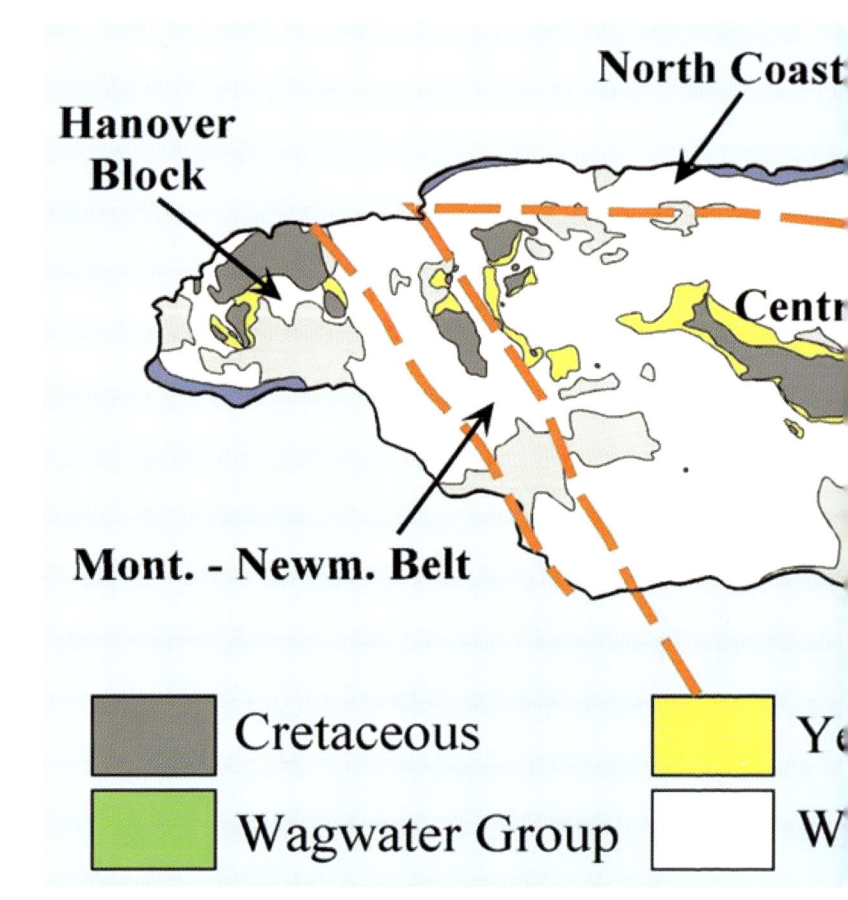

The Geology

of the Blue Mountains is important to the understanding of the geological evolution of Jamaica, being part of an ancient volcanic island (cf. St. Vincent). The oldest rocks are metamorphic rocks, exposed along the southern flanks of the Blue Mountains, and consist of schists and marbles formed at great depths in the Earth. Earlier geologists considered these rocks to be much older than any other rocks in Jamaica, but recent studies show that they may be Early Cretaceous.

In contrast, in the Bath, Dunrobin and Cedar Valley areas of the southeast Blue Mountains, limestones formed around the same time are fine-grained in character and are underlain by a suite of rocks indicating the presence of an ancient ocean floor (approximately 80 million years old). Geologists refer to this suite of rocks as an ophiolitic complex, consisting of chert, basalt and gabbro. Associated with these ophiolitic rocks are minor amounts of nickel, chromium and platinum.

The metamorphic rocks exposed along the southern flanks

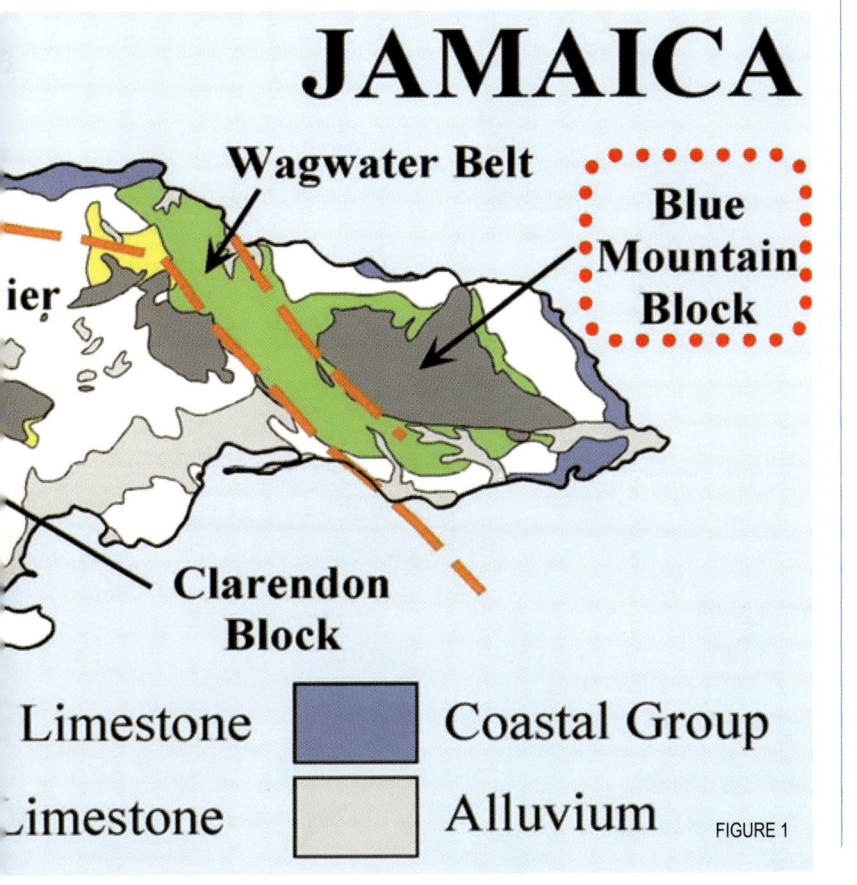

FIGURE 1

are in faulted contact with Campanian and Maastrictian (85 to 65 million years ago) lavas, sandstones and conglomerates. Associated with these rocks are minor beds of limestones containing an important group of fossils known as rudists (see Figure 2).

FIGURE 2

These rudist fossils belong to a group of bivalved molluscs which originated about 140 million years ago, and geologists can use them to date the rocks. These rocks are overlain by a thick pile of andesitic lavas in most of the central and northern Blue Mountains, which are capped by shallow-water limestones of Late Cretaceous age.

In other southern parts of the Blue Mountains, the Mahogany Vale and Jacob's Ladder area, thick sequences of sandstones and shales (see Figure 3) are overlain by coarse tuffaceous volcanic and conglomerate units.

FIGURE 3

Plutonic rocks (granites) found in the eastern Blue Mountains intrude Maastrictian rocks and are overlain by Paleocene limestones. This implies that the plutonism may have begun earlier in the Cretaceous.

The inlier is faulted along most of its eastern, southern and western margins. Geophysical evidence suggests that the major uplift which created this impressive landscape took place within the last 4 to 5 million years along the Blue Mountain–Plantain Garden Fault, which marks the southern margin of the inlier, and that the core is still imperceptibly rising. Thus the eastern section of the island, like much of the rest of Jamaica, is seismically active. Approximately 28 felt earthquakes with epicentres in Portland were recorded from 1977 through 1998.

There are numerous mineral springs located along these major fault zones (see Figure 4). One of the most used and well known of these springs is the Bath Spring in the parish of St. Thomas.

Commercial mining is limited to the Serge Island district in St. Thomas, where marble-type deposits are found along the

The Geology

FIGURE 4

southern and western sections of the inlier. Small-scale aggregate quarry sites can also be detected along the southern slopes of the inlier, as distinctive scars on the landscape.

Over the years, heavy rainfall, particularly during hurricanes, and the exploitation of woodlands within many of the southern and northern watersheds of the Blue Mountain Range have contributed to an increasing number of landslides, floods and soil erosion events. In 1937 a major landslide occurred along the southwestern slope of the John Crow Mountains, damming the Rio Grande for six months, inducing localised flooding and isolating the communities of Millbank and Comfort Castle.

The geology of the Blue Mountain Range is in many ways an important introduction to the geology of Jamaica, and this area is indeed one of the most impressive landscapes in the Caribbean.

THE JOHN CROW MOUNTAINS

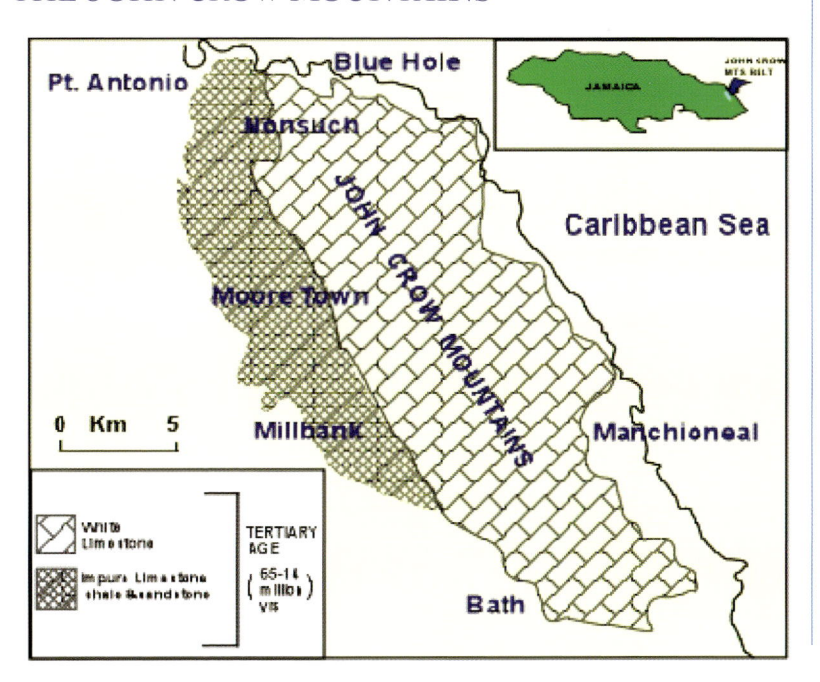

137

The John Crow Mountains (see Figure 5) extend over much of the parishes of Portland and St. Thomas and are composed largely of dense, recrystallised, poorly faulted white limestone. The extent of the white limestone in the John Crow Mountains exceeds 370 km2 as defined precisely by the first geological survey of Jamaica, summarised on a geological map of the whole island by Sawkins in 1869. However, there is no record of any detailed geology of the John Crow Mountains region. This is perhaps not surprising, as these mountains are renowned for their difficulty both of access and of traversing.

Geologists consider the white limestone to be of Tertiary age (14 – 50 million years).

On the southern peripheral parts of the John Crow Mountains, the white limestone is underlain by a more impure, sandy-textured limestone, also of Tertiary age but a bit older (50 to 60 million years). Geologists found that this limestone best outcropped in the Nonsuch area of Portland (see Figure 5) and therefore named it after the locality (Nonsuch Limestone). These limestones house one of Jamaica's famous karstic splendors, the Nonsuch Caves (see Figure 6).

This Nonsuch Limestone is underlain by shale and sandstone rocks, also of Tertiary age (60 – 60 million years). These rocks can be best seen in the Portland communities of Moore Town, Millbank and Comfort Castle. They support many waterfalls and springs that are ultimately drained by the Rio Grande. North of the community of Moore Town, nestled in the foothills of the John Crow Mountains,

FIGURE 6

FIGURE 7

Guide to the Blue and John Crow Mountains

flows one of Jamaica's majestic waterfalls, Nanny Falls, named after the famous Maroon leader and National Hero Nanny of the Maroons (see Figure 7). In this region of steep slopes, scarps and associated high rainfall, landslides and soil erosion are major occurrences. Geophysical evidence shows that this region of eastern Jamaica is seismically inactive.

SOURCES

de la Beche, H.T. 'Remarks on the Geology of Jamaica.' Transactions of the Geological Society of London, 2nd ser., 2, no. 20 (1827): 143–94.
Geologic Map of Jamaica, 1:250.000. Geological Survey Department. Provisional ed. (1958).
Sawkins, J.G. Reports on the Geology of Jamaica. Part II of The West Indian Survey: Memoirs. Great Britain Geological Survey, 1869. 339 pp.
McFarlane, N.A. Jamaica – Geology – 1:250,000. Kingston: Ministry of Mining and Natural Resources, 1977.

FURTHER READING

Anthony Porter Jamaica, A Geological Portrait (Kingston: Institute of Jamaica).

THE FLORA

Jim Dalling and Margaret Hodges

THE BLUE MOUNTAINS BY JIM DALLING

BEGONIAS

BROWALIA

Much of the beauty of the Blue Mountains can be attributed to the stunning diversity and intricacy of its forests – from moss-covered slopes to gullies filled with stands of primeval-looking tree ferns to the gnarled, stunted trees of the Peak. In total, there are more than 500 flowering plant species in the Blue Mountains, of which some 240, or nearly half, are unique to Jamaica.

Such diversity must have amazed the early botanists who visited Jamaica beginning in the late seventeenth century. Indeed, many of the plants of the Blue Mountains are described from that time. In recent years, the Jamaican flora has been more completely classified, with the publication of *The Flowering Plants of Jamaica* by C.D. Adams, *The Ferns of Jamaica* by G.R. Proctor and *A Guide to Plants in the Blue Mountains of Jamaica* by Sue Iremonger. The first two volumes should be consulted for detailed descriptions of plants. The third book is illustrated.

This chapter describes the changes in vegetation along the trail to Blue Mountain Peak, as well as some of the more common and interesting plants.

The Flora

FARMING

FOREST BOUNDARY

At one time the lower slopes of the Blue Mountains from Mavis Bank to Portland Gap were forested. Over the last two centuries, this has entirely changed. Coffee plantations and the cultivation of vegetables for the Kingston markets have taken over in part, but most areas have become a periodically burnt savannah of the highly combustible species wynne grass or molasses grass (*Melinis minutiflora*), introduced from Africa in about 1925. This grass is disliked by stock-keepers, as the tangled stems hide gullies and pitfalls from foraging animals – watch your step, too.

IRIS

THE BOUNDARY TO PORTLAND GAP

At lower altitudes in the Blue Mountains, much of the flora is composed of introduced species: along the path and in the grass, you will see the sky blue–flowered iris (*Aristea gerrardii*) from South Africa; *Calceolaria*, with yellow clam-shaped flowers, from Central America; and cheeseberry, the yellow-fruiting bramble from the Himalayas. Many were introduced as ornamentals and 'escaped' to the wilds. At Portland Gap, however, the ornamentals remain: beds of hydrangeas (seen again at the Peak), blue-flowering *Agapanthus*, red *Canna* lilies, *Fuchsias* and white *Arum* lilies.

141

PORTLAND GAP TO THE PEAK

From Portland Gap, as you move into more natural forest, the botanical richness increases markedly. Many herbaceous plants appear in the shade of the more complete tree canopy, and there are many more epiphytes on the trunks and branches of the trees themselves. An epiphyte is any plant that attaches itself to another plant for support, while herbs are defined as more or less non-woody plants. From here it is probably easiest to describe the most obvious elements of the flora in turn.

MOSSY BANK

SELAGINELLA

© A. HODGES

EPIPHYTES AND HERBS

MOSSES AND LICHENS

It's not difficult to see why botanists sometimes describe the Blue Mountains as 'moss forest'. In the more humid gullies, it seems as though every square inch of space is taken up – the trunks of the trees are coated in mosses, while the smaller branches of the trees' crowns are festooned with hanging filaments of the lichen *Usnea*.

ORCHIDS

There are at least 200 species of orchids in Jamaica, with about 65 species found in the Blue Mountains. The majority of these orchids are epiphytic, with very small flowers, sometimes not much larger than a pinhead. One of the most spectacular epiphytic orchids on the trail, often growing in clumps on low, hanging boughs of

Guide to the Blue and John Crow Mountains

The Flora

STELIS MICRANTHA

trees, is *Stelis micrantha*, which produces a mass of white flowers several times a year. The terrestrial (ground-dwelling) orchids are generally less conspicuous, but you may be fortunate enough to see the spectacular salmon-pink flowers of the Spiranthes speciosa early in the year, or the white-flowered *Prescottia stachyodes*.

BROMELIADS

These common epiphytes, known locally as wild pine, are closely related to the pineapple, and range in size from less than an inch to several feet in diameter, in the case of Hohenbergia and Guzmania. Like the epiphytes, they derive all the nutrients they need from the air and from the water that trickles down the branches of the trees on which they are anchored. Bromeliads are important components of the forest ecosystems. The spiralled arrangement of the leaves of many bromeliads traps water in a 'tank', providing water to the plant in periods of drought, and providing a home for many kinds of small animals.

FLOWERING BROMELIAD

FERNS

In addition to the many different types of epiphytic ferns – which range from the quite robust tongue-like fronds of *Elaphoglossum* to the very fine, single-cell-thick filmy ferns seen forming 'drapes' hanging from the bases of tree trunks – it's also common to

FERN GLADE
© ANDREW SMITH

143

BLECHNUM OCCIDENTALE

JOHN CROW BUSH

PILEA

see large patches dominated by terrestrial ferns. These are usually of the genus *Gleichenia*, a group of ferns which typically invade areas of the forest that have been disturbed by cutting or burning. Common on banks close to the path, and apparently adapted to the particular light conditions between the forest interior and the open, there are the downward-hanging pinkish fronds of *Blechnum occidentale*.

PATH-SIDE PLANTS

JOHN CROW BUSH

The straggling John Crow bush (*Bocconia frutescens*), with its large, hairy, pale-green lobed leaves, is a member of the poppy family. It sometimes reaches a height of 1.8 m (6 ft) or more. If you break off a leaf it will exude a bright orange sap, which is used in some countries as a dye or for medicinal purposes.

PILEA

There are two different-sized but otherwise very similar species of pilea, a non-stinging group of plants in the nettle family. The delicate crinkled leaves and attractive groups of tiny red flowers have made them popular house plants abroad.

The Flora

CUPHEA IGNEA

BLUE MOUNTAIN BEGONIA

CLIMBING BAMBOO

CIGAR BUSH

The cigar bush (*Cuphea ignea*), another escaped ornamental, blazes a trail from Portland Gap to the Peak. It's easy to see, from the shape and colour of its flowers, how it got its name.

BEGONIA

Often seen growing among rocks, the native species of begonia, *Begonia acutifolia*, has showy pink flowers present almost all year. There are thought to be at least 10,000 hybrids and varieties of begonias in cultivation around the world.

JAMAICAN BAMBOO

Although tall, cane-forming bamboo species have been introduced into Jamaica, there is a native bamboo, *Chusquea abietifolia*, which grows as a creeping vine and forms unpleasant prickly thickets, swamping all other vegetation beneath it. A remarkable feature of Chusquea is that all plants flower in synchrony, but only once every 33 years! This event was first reported in 1885, when it flowered both in Jamaica and at Kew Gardens in England. Chusquea last flowered in 1984, and is due again in 2017.

LOBELIA

There are several species of lobelia in the Blue Mountains, the most common of which is *Lobelia assurgens*, with scented pink tubular flowers. Note that the alkaloid-rich white sap is toxic.

TREES AND SHRUBS

TREE FERNS

Tree ferns (*Cyathea* spp.) are found in many of the wetter forests of Jamaica, but are seen at their best in the Blue Mountains. Like the related 'true ferns' mentioned earlier, they grow best in open disturbed areas, but they also thrive in some of the wetter gullies, where they are able to form almost pure stands. The curiously patterned trunks result from scars left when the leaves (fronds) drop off. By measuring the life of the fronds and counting the scars, botanists have estimated that some of the taller tree ferns may be up to 150 years old.

TREE FERN

SOAPWOOD OR CONEYWOOD

At lower altitudes *Clethra occidentalis* grows to about 15 m (50 ft) in height, while near the Peak it is replaced by the more densely hairy *Clethra alexandrii*. Both species of Clethra flower in August and September, producing clusters of small, sweet-scented, bell-shaped flowers, which are attended by the constant hum of visiting bees.

FLOWERING SOAPWOOD

JAMAICAN BILBERRY

Along the trail, and in disturbed forest, the Jamaican bilberry (*Vaccinium meridionale*) can reach 9 m (30 ft) in height. It is closely related to the tiny cranberry bush that grows in Europe and North America. In fact, the Jamaican bilberry produces a very similar edible fruit in July and August.

MELASTOMES

This group of tropical plants, well represented in the Blue Mountains, includes the spectacular cup-and-saucer (*Blakea trinerva*) and *Meriania purpurea*, with large deep-red pendulous flowers.

BLAKEA TRINERVA

SCHEFFLERA

UMBRELLA PLANT

Relatives of this small, straggling tree, *Schefflera sciadophyllum*, a member of the ivy family, are noted for their unusual foliage, consisting of compound leaves with individual leaflets arranged radially to form an umbrella shape.

YACCA

Looking across the slopes of the Blue Mountains from a vantage point on the trail, the tree you are most likely to see is the yacca (*Podocarpus urbanii*), related to the yew. This large tree, with smoothish, shaggy bark, is made more conspicuous by the very pale new flushes of foliage. Yacca can be recognised by its lance-shaped, stiff, leathery leaves. These leaves identify yacca as a cone-bearing tree, classified with the Gymnosperms – seed plants without true flowers or fruits but with exposed or 'naked' seeds.

PODOCARPUS (YACCA)

WILD COFFEE

Wild coffee (*Pittosporum undulatum*) is so named because its wavy leaf edges, fragrant white flowers and yellow fruit give it a resemblance to coffee. Wild coffee was introduced from

147

Australia at the end of the nineteenth century and cultivated in Cinchona Gardens. It has now spread across the forest and poses a considerable threat to the native flora, as it forms very dense and shady stands beneath which the native species are unable to survive.

CINCHONA

Cinchona trees from South America were cultivated in the Blue Mountains from 1860 as a source of quinine for the treatment of malaria. The initiative proved unprofitable and the plantations were abandoned, but occasional plants can be found in the forest.

BLUE MOUNTAIN PEAK

At the Peak itself, much of the vegetation has been altered by human disturbance. If hikers cut wood for fires, or fires damage the trees, it takes a very long time for regrowth to take place. This damage to the Peak is all the more tragic as the forest at the Peak itself is quite different from that of the slopes below. Ecologists have described it as 'elfin forest' because of the extremely low stature of the canopy, typically with trees less than 2.4 m (8 ft) in height. This forest is restricted in Jamaica to a small patch on Blue Mountain Peak, and patches on neighbouring High Peak and Mossman's Peak. The species present that are typical of this elfin forest are the densely hairy soapwood (*Clethra alexandrii*) and the very small-leafed rodwood (*Eugenia alpina*). The low stature of the forest on Blue Mountain Peak is probably a result of the extreme climatic conditions (the Peak is in fog much of the time, and under exceptional conditions the temperature drops below freezing).

Looking west from the Peak across the Grand Ridge to High Peak, it's possible to see the somewhat mysterious alpine meadows – patches of semi-natural grassland, pale green in contrast to the surrounding forest – composed of the tussock grass *Danthonia domingensis*. It has been suggested that this grass became established at the time of the last Ice Age; however, even if true, it is not clear how it has persisted to this day.

THE JOHN CROW MOUNTAINS
BY MARGARET HODGES

The John Crow Mountain range is a mass of limestone tilted from south to north. The highest area is 1,140 m (3,700 ft), near

JOHN CROW MOUNTAINS

the southern end. Near there it is bridged to the eastern slopes of the Blue Mountain range at Corn Puss Gap.

This mountain mass is the first high land reached by the easterly trade winds, and is consequently a very wet area. Flash rains and cloudbursts frequently occur, sending water rushing down dry riverbeds and disappearing into solution holes in the limestone. The thick forest cover, especially on the eastern side, reflects this heavy rainfall.

Paths run from Millbank in the north to Corn Puss Gap and link with other forest paths and tracks. One runs south to Bath in St. Thomas, and another reaches Hayfield. An easily accessible route into typical rainforest is from Johnson

ANTHURIUM

Mountain Village, where an old forestry track leads to the summit of Johnson Mountain. There is a steep but passable road from Wheelers Field to the village. There are tracks from the east through Windsor Forest and from Ecclesdown and Drivers River. A guide is necessary; it is easy to get lost and not easy to be found. There is no path or track leading all the way across the mountain, and at the top is a trackless wilderness with craggy limestone, deep solution holes and tangled vegetation. It is dominated in some areas by an endemic tree, *Clusia portlandia* (see below).

The diverse vegetation includes trees with climbers and epiphytes, herbs and shrubs, ferns, mosses, lichens and fungi. Some plants typical of the area are described in the following pages.

TREES AND SHRUBS

Typical of the area is the water mahoe (*Hernandia catalpifolia*), which grows to 20 m (65 ft) high and has a smooth grey trunk. The leaves are softly leathery and round, with an acute tip. The five main veins radiate from the base. The leaves are quite large, 37 x 26 cm (14 x 10 in). It is the food plant of the Jamaican Giant Swallowtail butterfly (*Pterourus homerus*, formerly *Papilio homerus*), the largest butterfly in the hemisphere, found only in Jamaica. The water mahoe is also endemic.

Clusia flava is a small tree or shrub which scrambles over the honeycombed limestone and the exposed roots of other trees. Its own roots resemble those of the red mangrove. The leaves are thick and fleshy, lighter green underneath. At high elevations the species is replaced by the endemic *Clusia portlandiana*.

OCHROMA TREE

Balsa or down tree (*Ochroma pyramidale*) is a fast-growing tall tree with light, spongy wood. The light yellowish-green leaves are rounded, 35 cm (14 in) in diameter. The balsa is often found near trumpet trees (*Cecropia peltata*), as both are indicative of disturbed forest. The trumpet tree is found all over the island, but the balsa needs more moisture and is therefore more restricted in its range.

Santa Maria (*Calophyllum calaba*) is often seen in small stands. It is tall and straight-trunked, grows to 40 m (130 ft) high, and has small, oblong, glossy leaves and woody, spherical fruits 2 cm (3/4 in) or so in diameter, often found scattered under the tree.

Broad thatch, long thatch and mountain cabbage are endemic palms which grow very well in the John Crow Mountains. It is interesting that the long thatch (*Calyptronoma occidentalis*) is also found in the Black River morass at sea level, and in the inland wetland at Mason River in Clarendon.

SANTA MARIA

Wild cinnamon or mountain cinnamon (*Cinnamodendron corticosm*) is a small tree with an aromatic bark. It is endemic to the John Crow Mountains at high elevations. The fairly narrow, pointed leaves are 5 to 12 cm (2 to 5 in) long, and the tiny red flowers grow from the leaf axils from June to August. The fruit is a small berry. Mountain cinnamon is related to the much more widespread *Canella* of dry forests.

EPIPHYTES, CLIMBERS AND HERBS

As already described, many of the trees carry bromeliads, orchids, ferns, mosses and lichens. Some other epiphytes may be members of the arum family, mostly originating from the Americas. Others of the family are climbers,

TERRESTRIAL AROIDS

and some are terrestrial. They are all characterised by their inflorescence, which is a fleshy spike surrounded at the base by a leaf bract known as a spathe. *Philodendron* and *Anthurium* species and Syngonium, or five-fingers, belong to this family. (Some are pollinated by flies and have a carrion-like odour.)

Many of the herbs and shrubs that grow near the path to Blue Mountain Peak, such as Melastomes and pileas, have their counterparts along these trails. Others are the spectacular yellow heliconias, little scarlet-flowering plants from the Gesneria family, ground orchids such as the white-flowering *Spiranthes elata*, and members of the pepper family. These have tiny greenish or white flowers on spikes, and when ripe can be used in the same way as black pepper, for seasoning food.

SPIKE AND SPATHE

SYNGONIUM

The John Crow nose (*Scybalium jamaicense*), illustrated, is a strange parasitic flowering plant which may grow in any damp woodland. It appears as a reddish clump of club-shaped organs which give rise to purplish male and female tiny flowers. The clumps may extend for several metres or more in the surface area of the leafy soil. This species parasitises tree roots.

JOHN CROW NOSE

LICHEN ON TREE

The Flora

FERNS IN BANK

FILMY FERNS

MAIDENHAIR FERN

FERNS

Ferns, mosses and liverworts grow in profusion, and many are endemic. Tiny ferns grow on the trees and hang from the branches. Others cover the ground, the limestone rocks and tree roots. Filmy ferns are small, delicate ferns, with fronds just one cell thick. They depend on mist and rain to keep them from drying out. Some hang from the bases of tree trunks and others grow on banks along streams. Most belong to the *Hymenophyllum* and *Trichomanes* genera.

Many ferns grow between the trees and shrubs, including maidenhair and strap ferns. The giant fern, *Angiopteris evecta*, is outstanding. It has fronds growing to 4 m (13 ft) or more, with bipinnate blades 3 m (10 ft) long and 2 m (6.5 ft) broad. It has stipules or swellings at the bases of the fronds, partly covering the thick root or rhizome. There is a cluster of these ferns near the source of the Rio Grande river, north of Corn Puss Gap, and others populate the southern slopes of Johnson Mountain. It has even spread to the Blue Mountain area and the hills near Hermitage dam. It is thought that they come from drifting spores from Castleton Gardens. The fern, originally described from Tahiti, was introduced to the gardens from the East Indies in the mid-nineteenth century. It is widely distributed in Southeast Asia, and in Hawaii it has been declared a noxious

GIANT FERN

weed. It is the largest fern in the world, but it is not a tree fern. Smaller related species grow naturally in Jamaica.

At least nine species of tree ferns have been recorded from the area of the John Crow Mountains. Some of these are tall and slender (up to 15 m tall – 50 ft – or more), but others are much shorter. One, with a very short trunk and numerous spines, is called macca fern, but nearly all the species have at least a few spines towards the leaf bases.

Other plants are described in the chapter describing specific areas of the park and its surroundings, especially in the eastern areas.

FIELD GUIDES

C.D. Adams *Flowering Plants of Jamaica* (Kingston: University of the West Indies Press,).
Susan Iremonger *A Guide to Plants in the Blue Mountains, Illustrated* (Kingston: University of the West Indies Press).
Tracey Parker *Manual of Dendrology – Jamaica* (Kingston: Jamaica Forestry Department, Department of Agriculture).
G.R. Proctor *Ferns of Jamaica* (UK: British Museum of Natural History).
Christopher Swaby *The Principal Timbers of Jamaica* (Kingston: Department of Agriculture).
Monica Warner *Flowers of Jamaica* (UK: Macmillan Caribbean).

THE FUNGI

Trevor Yee

Much of the area covered by the Blue and John Crow Mountains is prime habitat for mushrooms. After sufficient showers of rain, and especially in the rainy periods, mushrooms abound in river valleys, grassy areas, forests and trails. They are generally saprophytic; relatively few are parasitic. Some, especially the woody bracket types, will tolerate very dry conditions and remain in a dormant-like state on dead plant materials awaiting rains or misty weather, when they

ARTIST FUNGUS

will grow and produce spores in the comparatively short wet periods. *Ganoderma* spp. (Ganodermataceae) and *Fomes* spp. (Polyporaceae) are two such mushrooms. Both can be found in the dry limestone forests and on the drier southern slopes of the mountains in the park, and they will grow into large mushrooms over long periods of time, sometimes forming elaborate structures. Although these mushrooms are too woody and tough to eat, they can be interesting. *Ganoderma* spp., as its name means, has a shiny, often lacquered-looking top surface. One species, *G. applanatum*, has the common name 'artist fungus' because its flat white undersurface of pores invites writing or drawing on, and if one does mark on it, the outline darkens into a permanent etch. Some of these mushrooms also have remarkable powers of regeneration – if the cap is broken off, often a new one will slowly regrow.

In the wet periods, there are many locations where one can observe a wide variety of species. The hills and

SAFFRON MILKCAP

LAWN PUFFBALL

surrounding countryside of Holywell, Clydesdale, Cinchona and Guava Ridge are prime areas. In the grassy areas, many choice edible species, such as the meadow mushroom (*Agaricus campestris*), have been seen. The meadow mushroom is related to the imported button mushroom (*A. bisporus*), a strain of which, grown under special conditions, produces the large portobello mushroom. Other mushrooms grow in coniferous forests of, for example, Caribbean pine (*Pinus caribaea*). One of these is the edible saffron milkcap (*Lactarius deliciosus* [Russulaceae]), which has an orange sap that oxidises to a dark green, so that damage to the cap or gills results in a characteristic dark-green colour. Another of these coniferous forest–preferring species, also edible, is the slippery jack or sticky bun (*Suillus luteus* [Boletaceae]). This mushroom has a yellow cap with lemon-yellow pores underneath, and is slippery or sticky to the touch depending on the amount of moisture present. Before eating it, the slippery skin should be removed, as it can reportedly cause diarrhoea.

Several species of puffballs can also be found in these mountains. Among the edible species are the lawn puffball (*Vascellum pratense* [Lycoperdaceae]), a white spheroid 3 to 5 cm (1 to 2 in) in diameter, with small protuberances, seen in mown lawns after showers; the white to light-tan gem-studded puffball (*Lycoperdon perlatum* [Lycoperdaceae]), also found in grassy areas; and the pear-shaped white *L. pyriforme*, seen on

The Fungi

GIANT PUFFBALL

decayed wood. Especially after the October rains, the giant puffball (*Calvatia cyathiformis* [Lycoperdaceae]) is sometimes seen in grassy areas, while in the Guava Ridge area, where it appears to grow straight out of soil, is a poisonous genus, *Scleroderma* sp. (Sclerodermataceae). The name means thick skin, which is certainly apt, and the spore mass or gleba is dark-brown to black.

In St. Thomas and Portland, which experience heavy rainfall in the rainy seasons, many species can be observed. Around Millbank and near the Bath Fountain, the Botanical Gardens and surrounding areas can be found two beautiful mushrooms: the red cup fungus or Ascomycetes (*Cookiena sulcipes* [Sarcoscyphaceae]), considered less developed than the cap mushroom or Basidiomycetes, and the yellow staghorn fungus (*Calocera viscosa* [Dacrymycetaceae]). Little helmets or non-inky caps (*Coprinus disseminatus* [Coprinaceae]) also grow in abundance in these areas, in wet conditions.

RED CUP FUNGUS

In addition to morphology, one of the common aids to identification is a spore print. To make one, cut a freshly collected maturing cap at its junction with the stem and place it on a sheet of paper. Cover it to prevent air disturbing the dispersing spores, and leave it so that the developing spores can be deposited on the paper. The colour of the dispersed spores is a useful tool in identification.

YELLOW STAGHORN

The *Coprinus* spp. – many of which are edible, such as *C. micaceus*, with mica-like granules on top of the cap – do not allow a spore print to be taken, since they dissolve into an inky black mass of spores soon after collection. *C. disseminatus* – which, as its name implies, occurs in large numbers – is an exception. *C. atramentarius*, the alcohol inky, is notorious because after eating it, one cannot drink alcohol for up to two days; the combination causes severe intestinal disorders. The mechanism has been studied, and it has been found that the mushroom disturbs the breakdown of alcohol and produces undesirable amounts of harmful acetaldehyde.

COPRINUS DISSEMINATUS

The area around the Hermitage Dam is worth exploring in the rainy season. Observed there were a species of edible oyster mushroom, *Pleurotus djamor* (Tricholomataceae), appearing as white to off-white shelves, usually on dead tree trunks, and the wood ears (*Auricularia* polytricha [Auriculariaceae]), widely consumed in the Orient. In fact, in quite wet conditions in this area, both species were found growing all the way up on the bark of a living mango tree. A related species of *Auricularia* that is also widely consumed in the Far East, the Jew's ear fungus (*auricula-judae*), is frequently seen on the dead branches and twigs of mango trees, even around Kingston. This last mushroom is reported to be so named because it is commonly found on the branches of the elder tree, *Sambucus* sp.; legend has it that it was on this tree that Judas Iscariot hanged himself.

EDIBLE OYSTER MUSHROOM

AURICULARIA POLYTRICHA

It is essential to ensure a correct identification before consuming any wild mushroom. Individual tolerances can vary, so one should be cautious when tasting even a reportedly edible wild mushroom for the first time. It is also advisable to be cautious about consuming alcohol after eating wild mushrooms, as other mushrooms have been reported to have effects similar to the well-documented one caused by *Coprinus atramentarius*. Generally, one should always cook wild mushrooms, since some potential toxins are suspected to be destroyed by heat. Be aware, however, that the mushrooms described as poisonous are generally not detoxified by heat. Some mushrooms – for example, *Agaricus* spp. and *Auricularia* spp. – are considered safe enough to be consumed raw and are used in salads. Several poisonous species have been observed in the park. A fairly large mushroom that sometimes appears in large groups after rain showers in grassy areas is the green gill (*Chlorophyllum molybdites* [Agaricaceae]). The cap will grow to 30 cm (1 ft) in

CHLOROPHYLLUM MOLYBDITES (POISONOUS

CHLOROPHYLLUM MOLYBDITES, BUTTON STAGE

diameter, and these mushrooms emerge from the soil looking like large, off-white lollipops with a flaky brown skin. The gills start out white but later become a characteristic green when coloured by the developing spores. The spore print is green. This mushroom has been reported elsewhere to grow a cap as large as 1 m (3.2 ft). Another poisonous species seen at Holywell and in other areas of the Blue Mountains is the attractive *Russula emetica* (Russulaceae), with its red cap 3 to 8 cm (1 to 3 in) wide, and white stalk and gills. This mushroom occurs in wet, boggy areas of coniferous and mixed forests. Its common name is 'the sickener', since, as its name – emetic – implies, it will cause severe internal disorders.

THE SICKENER

So buy one of the many excellent books and field guides on mushrooms (several are listed below). Many of these have large numbers of photographs, with detailed descriptions for identification as well as information on which species are edible and which are not, where they are found and which other mushrooms are similar in appearance. Then, after periods of rain and being stuck indoors, venture out and look around the grass or in the forested areas, and you will be fascinated by the numerous types, forms and colours of the mushrooms that will be germinating from their spores.

MUSHROOM FIELD GUIDES

Colin Dickinson and John Lucas *The Encyclopedia of Mushrooms* (London: Orbis Publishing Ltd.).

Peter Jordon and Steven Wheeler *The Ultimate Mushroom Book* (London: Anness Publishing Ltd.).

Giuseppe Pace *Mushrooms of the World* (Ontario, Canada: Firefly Books Ltd.).

K. H. McKnight and V. B. McKnight *A Field Guide to Mushrooms. North America Peterson Field Guide Series* (Boston and New York: Houghton Mifflin Company).

G. H. Lincoff *National Audubon Society Field Guide to North American Mushrooms* (New York: Alfred A. Knopf).

THE INVERTEBRATES

Eric Garraway and Audette Bailey

PHOTOS BY AUDETTE BAILEY EXCEPT WHERE NOTED

THE BLUE MOUNTAINS

THE TRAIL AT NIGHT

CRICKET

BLINKY

KATYDID

If you climb at night, you can't miss the loud, piercing sounds of the crickets and the katydids. Why do they sing? They sing to attract mates. In some species of crickets, the male makes a burrow in the soil, then stands at the entrance and sings his heart out. The female listens to the many voices and then joins the best lyricist. They mate. She now occupies the burrow in which the eggs are laid. The male promptly moves on, makes another burrow and starts his singing again. Listen to their songs of short chirps. The katydids are large grasshoppers whose wings look like leaves. They make a loud shhhhh-shhhhhh.

You will also encounter the blinky and the peenywallie. These are both beetles that use light to attract mates. The more numerous of the two are the blinkies, *Lampyridae*, which are soft-bodied beetles about 5 to 15 mm (0.2 to 0.5 in) in length. Some species are light brown and others may be dark brown to black. They generate light via a chemical reaction which takes place in special organs located on the underside of the

PEENYWALLIE

last segments of the abdomen.

Every species has its own way of blinking – for example, long-short-long or short-short-long-long. Try to work out some of these 'blinking codes' as you climb. Watch out, too, for 'blinking trees'. Sometimes thousands of blinkies get together in a single tree and compete against each other; this is a spectacular sight, especially when they strike up the same rhythm. One carnivorous species blinks like the female of other species to attract unsuspecting males, who then get gobbled down.

The peenywallie (*Pyrophorus*) is a much bigger (25 mm, 1 in) and harder beetle than the blinky. The peenywallie has two sets of lights: a pair up front like small headlamps, and a single very bright one where thorax and abdomen meet, which is the one you will see as the beetle zooms around the hillside. Contrary to popular belief, these are not adult blinkies; the two are not related.

WALKING BY DAY

The insect life during the day is quite different. On your way down from the Peak you are bound to notice the honeybees. Honeybees are everywhere, and although they were originally introduced into Jamaica, they are the major pollinators in these forests. Honeybees pollinate both trees and herbs.

The butterflies are perhaps the largest insects on the trail. Only a small proportion of Jamaica's 120 species of butterflies are found here. Among the most common are the yellows and sulphurs.

CLOUDLESS SULPHUR

The *Eurema* is a common group: small bright-yellow and black or brown butterflies which have slightly more black or yellow depending on the time of the year. Perhaps the most interesting

Guide to the Blue and John Crow Mountains

The Invertebrates

butterfly is the Glass Wing (*Greta*), a small, fragile insect with wings like glass. Look for Vanessa the Virgin (*Vanessa virginiensis*), the American painted lady, basically orange with black, white, and gray markings, and two large eyespots on the underside of its hind wings. A moderate-sized, yellowish white butterfly is probably the Cabbage Butterfly (*Ascia*). The large Jamaican Giant Swallowtail (*Pterourus homerus*, formerly *Papilio homerus*) is not found on the southwestern approaches to the Peak but in the John Crow Mountains to the east.

Walking-stick and leaf insects have excellent camouflage – they look like bits of dried stick or yellow and green leaves. Some grow as long as 150 mm (6 in). These insects are harmless and feed on leaves and fruits.

A species of small black ant (*Crematogaster*) makes its nests in trees. This ingenious ant makes a nest like that of a termite (duck ants, white ants), but without tunnels extending away from the nest.

Many insects in the Blue Mountains live under the bark of dead trees, under stones and under dead leaves on the ground. A small disturbance will reveal the fast-running, spindly-legged ground beetles. These predators come in a variety of colours and are often iridescent.

The amphipods look like tiny dark shrimps lying on their sides – and they actually belong to the shrimp family. They are quick movers that appear to jump around.

Tunnel-web spiders are large spiders that use their webs to capture food in a simple but ingenious way. They make a funnel-shaped tunnel at the

GLASSWING

VANESSA THE VIRGIN

ANAEA TROGLODYTE

163

PELAUS SWALLOWTAIL

base of a tree or a bank. Unsuspecting insects seeking a place to hide climb into the tunnel – and into the spider's fangs. You will see many of these tunnels in the dry areas at the base of banks and trees.

The much smaller jumping spiders are also very common. These are very patient hunters that crawl up slowly to the unsuspecting foe; there is one final big jump, and the fly is caught in the fangs. The web is used as a safety line if the spider falls in the process.

There is a rich variety of land snails in Jamaica, and probably about 100 species live in the Blue Mountains. The numerous separate habitats formed by the rocks, the elevation and the humidity favour the development of different species. The shells most commonly seen are the large, round, slightly flattened ones of the *Pleurodonte* genus.

LIFE IN BROMELIADS

Rainwater collects in bromeliads, creating many tiny ponds in the forest. These are havens for animals that like water or very damp places. In fact, many depend on these ponds as a habitat for their larval stages. Often you will find:

- Various species of mosquitoes and the mosquito-like midges, which lay their eggs here.
- A small black beetle called *Colpodes*, which lives here in both adult and larval stages.
- Small bromeliad crabs
- Large crickets with very small wings, so that they have to depend on jumping.
- Some tree frogs who live in these 'ponds'.

BROMELIAD CRAB

© INSTITUTE OF JAMAICA

Guide to the Blue and John Crow Mountains

- A blue earthworm – blue because it has a copper-based chemical in its blood that helps to carry oxygen.
- Fast-running ground beetles, which find a lot of food here; they are often metallic-looking.
- Nymphs of needlecases (dragonflies and damselflies) that live in the water and feed on the larvae of smaller animals.
- Several slugs, which hide here during the heat of the day and feed at night when it is cool.

THE JOHN CROW MOUNTAINS

BUTTERFLIES

Most of the butterflies are readily seen along the margin of the forest. They are often feeding on a range of flowers and rotting fruits.

The milkweed butterflies, of which the Monarch is the best known, lay their eggs on the underside of leaves of *Euphorbia* species or of red head (*Asclepias curassavica*), which has a poisonous milky sap. There are three other members of the genus Danaus that live in Jamaica, smaller and varying in colour and pattern. Mostly with a similar orange-brown colour with blackish edgings and white spots. They can be seen throughout the year. You may see the Common Dusky Brown (*Calisto zangis*), with a wingspread of about 4 cm (1.5 in). It is a slow flyer and flies low among the vegetation.

Butterflies seen feeding on rotting fruits on the ground are the handsome Malachite (*Siproeta stelnes*), a malachite-green and black

MILKWEED

DANAUS GILLIPUS

DANAUS PLEXIPPUS

165

butterfly, not easily scared away; another large reddish-orange butterfly, Orion (*Historis odius*); and a similar darker one, H. *acheronta calmus*, with some white spots on the upper wing. These feed on fruit and are sometimes seen flying among the trees or on the ground.

MALACHITE

The Banana butterfly, *Colobura dirce* is a fast flyer. It often sits on tree trunks with wings closed, and its cream underside with a complex pattern of brown makes it well camouflaged and difficult to spot. When it opens its wings there is a broad yellow band diagonally across its forewing while the rest is dark brown. Buckeye (*Junonia evarete*), another brown butterfly, is easily identified by the prominent eyespots on both wings and is very common among the flowers of shrubs.

BANANA BUTTERFLY

Two species that feed on passionfruit vines (*Passiflora* sp.) are the Zebra (*Heliconius charitonius simulator*), with its bright-gold and black stripes, and a bright-orange member of the same family that is often observed flying fast among nectar sources.

Several species of small blue and green butterflies, some with small, hairlike tails on the hind wings, can be seen flying lazily in sunny spots.

The Swallowtails are well represented in the John Crow Mountains; they are generally yellow and black or brown. They are large butterflies compared with the others, with wingspreads from 4.5 cm (1.7 in)

ZEBRA BUTTERFLY

THERSITES SWALLOWTAIL

GIANT SWALLOWTAIL

in the case of *Battus polydamus jamaicensis* and 15 cm (6 in) for the largest Swallowtail in the Americas, *Pterourus homerus*, usually known as *Papilio homerus*. This beautiful butterfly is now an endangered species, partly because so much tree cover in Jamaica has been cut for cultivating or charcoal burning, and partly as a result of butterfly hunting for and by collectors. With the National Park in place, and laws against the removal of endangered species, we hope it will survive. Even now, it is not too uncommon to see it flying lazily above streams in areas such as Millbank and Johnson Mountain.

OTHER INVERTEBRATES

LADYBUG

Like the crickets and katydids, cicadas make loud shrills. They are common from May through July and are called July pipers. They are difficult to find among the shrubs, which are frequent along the margins of the forest. Cicadas, black with transparent wings, are 4.5 to 5 cm (1.7 to 2 in) long. Adults are often heard and not seen, but the translucent nymph cases are often visible, hanging from the stems of trees and shrubs.

Small (1 cm) black and red ladybugs are commonly seen in large numbers, in all stages of development, on shrubs on the forest margin. Very often adults are seen mating.

The praying mantis, or god-horse, as it is sometimes called,

167

PRAYING MANTIS

is not always distinguished by name from the stick insect. Mantises, which are uncommon, are generally green or brown. When a praying mantis is disturbed, it stretches out its wings and displays the bright pink near the base of the wings. This is a warning colouration that protects them from predators. They are 7.5 cm (about 3 in) long.

The police bug or policeman (*Exophthalmus vittatus*) is a common resident, often seen in large numbers. These colourful insects are striped in combinations of black and red, blue and black or any combination of these colours. The red stripes call to mind those on Jamaican policemen's trousers. They can be seen feeding on shrubs or on the ground.

If you see a large number of shiny black beetles about 3 cm (1 in) long feeding on the flowers of forest trees or on fruits such as otaheite apple or rose apple, they are probably *Macropsis tetradactyla*.

The silk cotton beetle (*Euchroma gigantea*) is rare, but its iridescent greenish-purple wings and large size (5 to 5.5 cm, around 2 in) distinguishes it from all other beetles. It is the largest beetle in Jamaica, and its caterpillars feed on the bark of the silk cotton tree. It should never be collected!

The shiny black wasp (*Campsomeris atrata*) is 3 cm (1 in) long and has a pointed abdomen and brown irridescent wings. These wasps can be seen feeding on the inflorescence of shrubs in the forest undergrowth or on shrubs such as bastard

SILK COTTON BEETLE

The Invertebrates

PERIPATUS

vervine (*Stachytarpheta* sp.) along the margin of the forest.

An interesting invertebrate found in the John Crow Mountains is the halfway animal, peripatus. The species *Plicatoperipatus jamaicensis* and *P. swainsonae* measure 5.5 to 6.5 cm (2 to 2.5 in). *P. jamaicensis* is reddish-brown whereas *P. swainsonae* is greenish. They are uncommon but have been found in the forest around Bath. They live in dark, moist places, such as under leaf litter, stones and logs. They have short, wormlike bodies that are velvety in appearance. They are called halfway animals because they have features characteristic of different animal groups, in particular annelids (to which earthworms belong) and insects, and other features of their own. The antennae are characteristic of insects, but the clawed, paired feet are unlike those found in other phyla. They have therefore been placed in a phylum of their own, Onychophora.

FIELD GUIDES

F. Martin Brown and **Bernard Heineman** *Jamaica and its Butterflies* (London: E.W. Classey).
Ralph Buchsbaum *Natural History Notes: Animals without Backbones* (Cincinnati: Museum of Natural History).
E. Garraway and A. Bailey *Butterflies of Jamaica* (Macmillian).

THE VERTEBRATES

Thomas Farr

This chapter was written for the Blue Mountain Guide in 1993 by Dr Thomas Farr of the Institute of Jamaica, who unfortunately died in 1996. It did not include the coney or the wild pig, as they are found more often in the limestone John Crow Mountains. The escaped white-tailed deer had not yet become a part of the forest fauna, so notes on these three species have been added.

REPTILES

Twenty-five species of lizard are known in Jamaica, but only three are likely to be found at altitudes of 1,220 m (4,000 ft) and higher. Two of these species belong to the genus *Anolis*. Most commonly seen is *Anolis opalinus*, the coffee lizard, which is widely distributed on the island. Its total length, from nose to tail, is about 100 mm (4 in), and it is dark in colour, mostly shades of olive-brown or grey, with a white stripe extending from the head along each side of the body.

Anolis reconditus is common in the Hardwar Gap region and may also be found around Blue Mountain Peak. Its total length is about 225 mm (9 in), and it is a dull grayish-green colour with a broad lighter stripe on the back. Any rather large greenish-grey lizard resting on a shrub or clinging to a tree trunk along the trail will probably be an *A. reconditus*.

There is a little gecko lizard found in the mountains, even on Blue Mountain Peak (according to one herpetologist, Barbour 1910). This is *Sphaerodactylus goniorhynchus*, which also occurs at lower elevations down to sea level. It is quite small, about 50 mm (2 in) in length, mostly dark brown with a light band on each side of the body. You are not likely to see this species unless you search through leaf litter or under logs.

Two other lizard species have been reported from localities of about 1,220 m

SPHAERODACTYLUS
© ANN SUTTON

(4,000 ft), and it is possible that they could move higher up. One is a bright-green species with a saw-toothed ridge on the back. This is *Anolis garmani*, sometimes called 'guana' or 'Venus', which may be nearly 300 mm (1 ft) in length. The other is *A. lineatopus*, the bush lizard, a tan or brown species patterned with dark brown, common in the lowlands.

If you are afraid of snakes, don't be apprehensive about meeting one while hiking along Blue Mountain trails, as there are no records of snake species occurring at higher altitudes.

VENUS LIZARD

AMPHIBIANS

The frog genus *Eleutherodactylus* is well represented in the American tropics, and 19 species occur in Jamaica. The generic name is a compound of two Greek words, 'free' and 'fingers', and was applied to the group because the toes of the hind feet are not webbed, except in a few species. The members of this genus lay their eggs on land in moist situations, and the tadpoles complete their development within the egg, hatching out as frogs.

Of our 19 species of *Eleutherodactylus*, 17 are endemic, two have been introduced, one deliberately and the other accidentally, and one Jamaican species has been accidentally introduced to Bermuda. The frogs of this genus are small, from a little less than an inch (25 mm) to an inch and a half (38 mm) in length, and are coloured in dull shades of brown and grey, sometimes with a pinkish cast. They are mostly nocturnal, spending the day in or beneath logs, under rocks or hidden in the leaf litter of forests. Some of them can produce a call, which has been described as a chirp. Eight species have been found in the Blue Mountains, of which only two are mentioned here, E. alticola and *E. nubicola*. Both of these are apparently confined to higher altitudes,

E. NUBICOLA

E. nubicola from 1,070 to 1,830 m (3,500 to 6,000 ft) and E. alticola from 1,070 m to Blue Mountain Peak at 2,257 m (3,400 to 7,400 ft).

One other species of frog lives in the Blue Mountains, a tree frog, *Osteopilus brunneus*, (formerly *Hyla brunnea*). *O. brunneus* is the most widespread of the four species of tree frogs in Jamaica. An endemic species, it has been found from certain areas near sea level to about 1,500 m (5,000 ft) in the mountains. This frog is nearly 75 mm (3 in) long and is capable of considerable colour change, ranging from very dark brown to light grey. The back may be marked with dark and light blotches, and the hind legs may have a series of transverse stripes. The eggs are laid in water trapped in wild pines (Bromeliads), often in large numbers. Also living in the water are insects and other small forms of plant and animal life, which the tadpoles can feed on. However, the potential number of tadpoles hatching from the eggs would be too great to be supported by the food supply available, so the earlier-hatching tadpoles eat the unhatched eggs.

WILD PINE

MAMMALS

Apart from the occasional goat or donkey and various human specimens sighted along the way, you will find few mammals on the trail to the Peak. An exception is the mongoose, which may be seen flashing across your path as high as the Peak.

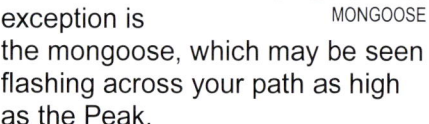

Of Jamaica's 22 native mammals, all but one, the Jamaican hutia or coney (probably not present in the Blue Mountain Peak region),

YOUNG MONGOOSES

MONGOOSE

The Vertebrates

are bats ('rat bats'). Unfortunately, there is little documentation of bat sightings in the Blue Mountains. *Tadarida brasiliensis murina*, one of the two long-tailed species of bats found in Jamaica, has been found at Hardwar Gap and also at Whitfield Hall, near the start of the trail. It is the only species documented in this area, though certainly others may occur.

BAT

JAMAICAN HUTIA OR CONEY

The Jamaican coney survives in the John Crow Mountains as well as in a few other isolated hills, such as in Hellshire. It is a large grey rodent, weighing up to 2.5 kg (5.5 lb). It is unlikely to be seen, as it is nocturnal and makes its burrows in the rocky limestone, full of solution holes and small caves.

CONEY

Coneys eat a variety of plant foods, and are themselves preyed on by owls and the mongoose. Stray cats and dogs may also hunt them, as do men, illegally. Its numbers have declined, but with protection within the park and stricter law enforcement, the coney could be saved.

WILD HOGS

There are also wild hogs, descendants of the domestic hogs brought in by the Spanish settlers in the fifteenth century. Small packs are found in remote forested areas such as the east Portland–John Crow

WILD HOG

area, as well as in Hellshire, St. Catherine and the western and northern sections of the park. They too are hunted from time to time illegally, by men with dogs.

WHITE-TAILED DEER

White-tailed deer (*Odocoilens virginianus*) may possibly be seen in the northern forests of the Blue Mountains and in the John Crow Mountains.

In 1988 hurricane Gilbert swept through the island, and some deer escaped from a private property in Portland. Since then their numbers have increased, and they may become a problem for small farmers. They have no cold winter to contend with, and no enemies except hunters to restrict their increase.

WHITE-TAILED DEER

Adults stand 90 to 100 cm (3 to 3.5 ft) at the shoulder and weigh 56 to 90 kg (125 to 200 lb). The males are larger than the females. They are reddish-brown, with white fur in a band behind the nose, around the eyes, inside the ears and over the chin and throat. The underside of the tail is markedly white, and the tail is held up like a flag when the animal is alarmed or running. Mature males grow a pair of spiked antlers which they lose after the autumn mating season and grow again in the spring.

The young, called fawns, have a reddish and white dappled coat. They are born in the early summer, usually one or two to each female, or doe. Each mother looks after her own, hiding them in the bush while she forages for food. She nurses them for several months, although they also nibble leaves as soon as they can stand and move. They can run a week after birth. When in the hide, they withhold faeces and urine until the mother returns. She ingests these to avoid any smell that might attract predators. When weaned, the fawns stay with the does in a group; the males leave as they mature, up to two years. Mating takes place in the autumn.

Although the deer are shy and unlikely to be seen, their spoor is sometimes seen after wet weather. The male print is about 8.5 (3.3 in) cm long, and the hoofprints of the does and fawns are smaller.

The Vertebrates

STREAMERTAIL FEMALE FEEDING YOUNG

THE BIRDS OF THE MOUNTAIN AREA

Catherine Levy and Marcia Mundle

The clear, sustained notes of the Rufous-throated Solitaire (*Myadestes genibarbis*) are evocative of the Blue Mountains. Many of Jamaica's endemic bird species (that is, those found exclusively in Jamaica) are to be found in mid- and high-level forests. Of the 113 breeding birds on the island, 26 are endemic species and 20 are endemic subspecies. In addition, there are nearly 100 migrants from the north that spend the winter months here, some staying for as long as eight months. Most of these birds are dependent on the natural forest, which is being or has been encroached upon by plantations growing coffee or Caribbean pine, by removal of trees for charcoal burning and by small-scale farming. The widespread clearing of land has opened up habitats for birds that are not forest-dependent.

SOLITAIRE © H VAUGHN

Some of the less commonly seen birds typical of mid- to high-level forests are briefly described. All birds mentioned are listed at the end of the chapter for further reference. Size refers to length from bill to tail end.

BIRDS OF MID- TO HIGH-LEVEL FORESTS

RUFOUS-THROATED SOLITAIRE

The Solitaire (19 cm, 7.5 in) is a member of the thrush family. It is recognised by the white crescent under the eye and the white chin, and by the rufous throat. Most of the colouring is grey – head, back, wings and tail dark, and breast light. There is also some rufous colouring of the undertail coverts and the white outer feathers to the tail. The most outstanding feature is the call, a long, flute-like whistle followed by another harmonising with it. In summer, trills are sometimes added.

JAMAICAN BLACKBIRD

The Jamaican Blackbird (18 cm, 7 in) is sometimes called the Wild-pine Sargent because of its habit of foraging in wild pines (Bromeliads) for insects. It is our most endangered species, being restricted to mature mountain forests. It is a shiny black bird with a sharp, pointed bill and has a loud, rattling, wheezy call. It is found only in Jamaica.

JAMAICAN BLACKBIRD

CRESTED QUAIL DOVE

This bird (30.5 cm, 12 in) is also called the Mountain Witch. It is a colourful dove that lives mostly in the undergrowth in the Blue and John Crow Mountains. One or two together are sometimes seen walking on a forest path, foraging in the leaf litter, or flying short distances near to the ground, sometimes roosting higher in a tree. The head and breast are grey, including the short crest. The upper back and wings are rufous and magenta, the lower back an iridescent greenish-black, and the underparts rufous. Like all members of the pigeon family in Jamaica, its legs are reddish.

MOUNTAIN WITCH

RING-TAILED PIGEON

The protected endemic Ring-tailed Pigeon (40.5 cm, 16 in) is a large, light-grey bird with a marked black band across the middle of its long tail. It lives in small flocks high in the trees of the Blue and John Crow Mountains.

RING-TAILED PIGEON

WHITE-EYED THRUSH

This thrush (23 cm, 9 in) is sometimes called Glass Eye or Shine Eye. The head is a rich brown colour from which the yellowish-white eye 'shines out'. The breast is light grey with a white band at the foreneck. The back is brown and black. It feeds on fruit and insects from treetops to ground level and is sometimes seen in shrubbery by the roadside.

BIRDS ALSO SEEN IN OTHER PARTS OF THE ISLAND

DOCTOR BIRD

RED-BILLED STREAMERTAIL AND BLACK-BILLED STREAMERTAIL

The males of these two closely related hummingbirds measure 22 to 24 cm (8.5 to 9.5 in) including their long tail plumes, (giving them their name, Doctor Bird, after the tail-coats of early doctors). The females have short tails and are only 10.5 cm (4 in) long. The Red-billed Streamertail is Jamaica's national bird. It is found from sea level to the top of Blue Mountain Peak and throughout the west of the island. In the John Crow Mountains and the east, the Black-billed Streamertail is dominant and is quite often encountered. These species overlap

FEMALE STREAMERTAIL

YOUNG STREAMERTAILS

on the western side of the John Crows. The Black-billed is slightly smaller than the Red-billed but is otherwise very similar, feeding on nectar and small insects and making its tiny nest from plant fibres and cobwebs, moss and lichen.

JAMAICAN TODY

The Tody (9 cm, 3.5 in) is sometimes called Robin Redbreast or Rastabird. It is mostly leaf-green except for its bright-red throat and the lower mandible of its long bill and white breast washed with pale green and yellow. It is not at all shy, and is often seen near trails, sitting under a shrub with head tilted up, searching for insects on the underside of leaves. It flies up and from one perch to another with a whirring sound. It is a distant relation of the Kingfisher, and nests at the end of a burrow in a bank of earth, or in a rotten tree trunk.

JAMAICAN TODY

JAMAICAN WOODPECKER

The Woodpecker (24 cm, 9 in) attracts attention by tapping on tree trunks and branches, and by

JAMAICAN WOODPECKER

179

its loud cry. When it is moving up and down trees, the red crown and nape of the neck, cream face, and mainly black back, wings and tail can be seen. The breast is brownish.

CHESTNUT BELLIED CUCKOO

CHESTNUT-BELLIED CUCKOO

Locally this bird (56 cm, 22 in) is called Old Man Bird, or Hunter. It is found in woodlands at altitudes from 400 to 1,500 m (1,300 to 4,900 ft). It is a striking bird with a tail barred with white-tipped feathers. The head and back are dark grey, the throat and chest light grey (the 'beard' of the Old Man). The belly and underparts are a dark chestnut-brown. It has a strong curved bill. It may move softly from tree to tree and then rapidly along branches to snatch insects or lizards – and sometimes birds' eggs or nestlings – for food. The call is a guttural, accelerating 'quawk – quawk – ak – ak – ak' sound.

ORIOLE

The Jamaican Oriole (21 cm, 8 to 9 in) known as Aunt Katie, is greenish yellow, becoming a brighter yellow in spring, with a black mask and white patch on the wings. It has a strikingly loud and melodious song including a phrase sounding like 'sea view, sea view'.

JAMAICAN ORIOLE

WHITE CROWNED PIGEON

The White crowned pigeon (35 cm, 14 in) is commonly known as Bald Pate. It is grey overall except for the crown, which in males is white, and in females and young birds grayish white. It is usually with others, sometimes in a large flock.

BALD PATE

Guide to the Blue and John Crow Mountains

BULLFINCH

The Greater Antillean Bullfinch (16 cm, 6 to 7 in) has a thick bill. It is black with a chestnut red stripe over the eye, on the throat and under the tail. The female is brownish grey and the red less prominent. They move quietly in shrubbery and trees searching for fruits and seeds, and also snails.

BULLFINCH

EUPHONIA

The Jamaican Euphonia (11.5 cm, 4.5 in) known as Blue Quit is a small bird with a short dark bill, the male grayish blue with yellow under parts. The female head and under parts are bluish, the back and wings an olive green. It often forages in flocks, feeding on shoots, buds and fruits of trees. Mistletoe berries depend on it for seed dispersal.

EUPHONIA

FLYCATCHERS

There are many different species of flycatcher in forest areas. One of the largest and commonest is the Loggerhead Kingbird (20.5 cm, 8 in). The upper part of the head, the bill, the back, the wings and the back of the tail are black, and the whole front of the bird below the bill is white. It boldly flies out to catch insects and back to its perch.

Another is the Rufous tailed flycatcher (24 cm, 9.5 in) with its distinctive chestnut colour on wings and tail.

RUFOUS TAILED FLYCATCHER

BECARD

The Becard (18 cm, 7 in) is a small flycatcher. The male is black, glossy above and duller below, whereas the female and immature have a rufous-brown head, upper breast and wings, with the breast shading to light grey below.

Between March and June each pair builds an enormous nest hanging from the end branches of a tall tree. The nest, composed of grass, ferns, vines, leaves and moss, is sometimes a metre long. They enter it from below. Sometimes a number of pairs build near to each other.

BECARD ON NEST

FEMALE BECARD"

ORANGEQUIT

Male Orangequits (14 cm, 5.5 in) appear blue when seen in sunlight and blue-grey in shade. They do have an orange patch on the throat. They are great fruit eaters and also take nectar. They are often seen along the roads near Holywell.

ORANGEQUIT

WHITE-CHINNED THRUSH

The White-chinned Thrush (24 cm, 9.5 in), usually called Hopping Dick, is found all over the island. Any dark-grey to

HOPPING DICK

black bird with a bright-orange bill and legs, hopping along the road, cocking up its tail as it pauses, is a Hopping Dick. It has a white spot on the chin and a more visible one on the wing. It has a beautiful rich song and can also utter a shrill alarm call. Sometimes it clucks like a hen. It feeds on berries, insects and small lizards.

BIRDS OF THE JOHN CROW MOUNTAINS

JAMAICAN CROW

The Jamaican Crow (38 cm, 15 in) is normally called the Jabbering Crow because of its loud, raucous 'caw-caw' and jabbering. Often in a flock, crows fly slowly and feed on invertebrates, especially those in bromeliads.

PARROTS, PARAKEETS AND THE PARROTLET

YELLOW-BILLED PARROT

Parrots, Parakeets and the small Parrotlet are found more often in the John Crow Mountains than on the western and southern slopes of the Blue Mountains. Flocks of green birds, flying sometimes very high in the sky and making high-pitched squawks, are either parrots (birds with short tails) or parakeets (birds with long tails). Populations of parrots are threatened by collection for the pet trade and by habitat destruction.

The Olive-throated Parakeet (30.5 cm, 12 in) is a slim, mainly green bird with a dark olive-brown throat, breast and abdomen. It has a long, pointed black tail, and the bill is pale horn-coloured.

BLACK-BILLED PARROT

When seen at close quarters, the Yellow-billed Parrot (26.5 cm, 10.5 in) is easily distinguished from the Black-billed Parrot by its colouring. The Yellow-billed Parrot is green overall with a yellow bill and legs, white forehead and eye rings, bluish head and maroon throat and base of tail. The Black-billed is entirely green with a black bill and greyish feet. Both feed on fruits and seeds.

Green-rumped Parrotlets (13 cm, 5 in) are tiny, short parrotlets. Mostly green, the males have bluish patches on wings and rump while the females have a yellowish breast. They travel in noisy flocks, feeding on grass seed and small fruits and blossoms. They may nest in tree holes or caves.

ANI

The Smooth-billed Ani (35 to 40 cm, 14 to 15 in) is a shrill, long-tailed black bird with a parrot-like bill. It is often seen in small noisy flocks on the ground or in low bushes.

ANI

Guide to the Blue and John Crow Mountains

BIRDS OF PREY

Birds of prey, such as the American Kestrel and Red-tailed Hawk, are seen in more open, cultivated areas, and in winter months the Merlin and Osprey may also be seen. At the eastern end of the island the distance from south to north across the island is approximately 32 km, 20 miles as the Osprey flies, and so it is never far from the sea.

RED-TAILED HAWK

The John Crow or Turkey Vulture, found all over Jamaica, may also be seen circling in the sky, usually with others, on the lookout for carrion. It is a large bird, more than 63 cm

JOHN CROW

(25 in) long, and soars with its two-toned black wings in a V shape above its head. When on the ground, feeding, its red, featherless neck and head are visible. Turkey Vultures sometimes gather in a tree or on a roof and stand in the sun with their wings spread.

John Crow was the name of an Irish clergyman who made himself very unpopular with the slaves. In revenge they called the Turkey Vulture 'John Crow'. With its red head and black 'gown' of feathers this was apt and caught on. Until 1826 the eastern mountains were named 'Carrion crow hills' but they then became 'John Crow Mountains'. The red 'John Crow nose' pictured in the eastern flora, and the poisonous red and black John Crow beads must also owe their names to this incident.

MIGRANTS

In winter, late August to April or May, numbers of migrant wood warblers may be seen, especially the American Redstart, the Black-throated Blue Warbler and the Black-and-White Warbler. This last should be distinguished from the endemic Arrow-headed Warbler, but both are known locally as 'Ants-picker'. Among other North American migrants to be seen are the Rose-breasted Grosbeak and the Yellow-bellied Sapsucker.

PRAIRIE WARBLER

BLACK WHISKERED VIREO, LOCAL NAME JOHN CHEWIT

From the north of South America, the Black Whiskered Vireo (15 to 16.5 cm, 5.75 to 6.5 in) flies up to the Caribbean to nest, returning in September. They usually arrive in March or April, filling the hills and valleys with loud and repetitive song 'John Chewit, Sweet John, John Chewit'. The distinguishing marks are well shown in the photograph, the eye stripe, the black whisker and general colouring.

BLACK-WHISKERED VIREO

JAMAICAN BIRDS FOUND AT MIDDLE AND HIGH ALTITUDES

Cattle Egret
Turkey Vulture
Red-tailed Hawk
American Kestrel
White-crowned Pigeon
Ring-tailed Pigeon*
Zenaida Dove
Common Ground Dove
Crested Quail Dove*
Ruddy Quail Dove
Jamaican Parakeet
Yellow-billed Parrot*
Black-billed Parrot*
Jamaican Lizard Cuckoo*
Chestnut-bellied Cuckoo*
Smooth-billed Ani
Barn Owl
Jamaican Brown Owl*
Black Swift
White-collared Swift
Antillean Palm Swift
Red-billed Streamertail*
Black-billed Streamertail*
Vervain Hummingbird
Jamaican Tody*
Jamaican Woodpecker*
Jamaican Elaenia*
Greater Antillean Elaenia
Greater Antillean Peewee
Sad Flycatcher*
Rufous-tailed Flycatcher*
Jamaican Becard*

Loggerhead Kingbird
Grey Kingbird†
Golden Swallow
Jamaican Crow*
Rufous-throated Solitaire
White-chinned Thrush*
White-eyed Thrush*
Northern Mockingbird
Jamaican Vireo*
Blue Mountain Vireo*
Black-whiskered Vireo†
Arrow-headed Warbler*
Bananaquit
Orangequit*
Jamaican Euphonia*
Stripe-headed Tanager
Black-faced Grassquit
Yellow-shouldered Grassquit*
Greater Antillean Bullfinch
Jamaican Blackbird*
Jamaican Oriole

_____

*Indicates birds endemic to the island.
†The Black-whiskered Vireo and the Grey Kingbird are summer residents, coming in spring to breed and returning home at the end of the summer.

NORTH AMERICAN MIGRANTS THAT HAVE BEEN FOUND AT MIDDLE AND HIGH ALTITUDES IN THE BLUE MOUNTAINS

Merlin
Osprey
Tree Swallow
Yellow-bellied Sapsucker
Veery
Grey-cheeked Thrush
Swainson's Thrush
Grey Catbird
Philadelphia Vireo
Red-eyed Vireo
Yellow-throated Vireo
Eastern Wood Peewee
Summer Tanager
Palm Warbler
Prairie Warbler
Tennessee Warbler
Northern Parula
Bay-breasted Warbler
Black-and-White Warbler
Black-throated Blue Warbler
Black-throated Green Warbler
Blackburnian Warbler
Yellow-throated Warbler
Cape May Warbler
American Redstart
Worm-eating Warbler
Ovenbird
Common Yellowthroat
Louisiana Waterthrush
Chestnut-sided Warbler
Swainson's Warbler
Blue-winged Warbler
Nashville Warbler
Blackpoll Warbler
Cerulean Warbler
Rose-breasted Grosbeak
Northern Oriole
Cedar Waxwing
Lincoln's Sparrow
White-winged Crossbill

RECOMMENDED GUIDEBOOKS

A. Downer and R. Sutton *Birds of Jamaica, A Photographic Field Guide Photographs by Yves-Jacques Rey-Millet* (Cambridge: Cambridge University Press).

National Geographic Society Field Guide to the Birds of North America (Washington, DC: National Geographic Society). (Or any other field guide to North American birds east of the Rockies, for migratory warblers and other birds common to both countries.)

Herbert Raffaele, Orlando Garrido, James Wiley, and others *Birds of the West Indies* (Princeton: Princeton University Press).

LIFE IN STREAMS AND RIVERS

Kimberly John and Eric Hyslop

Several of Jamaica's well-known rivers originate as springs in the Blue and John Crow Mountains National Park. These rivers account for more than half of the total volume of surface water resources in Jamaica. Those draining the northern slopes of the mountains (Rio Grande, Spanish, Swift, Buff Bay and Wagwater rivers) receive more rainfall and therefore discharge more water than those on the southern slopes. The Hope, Yallahs, and Morant rivers drain the drier slopes of the Blue Mountains. The Plantain Gardens, Drivers, and Priestman rivers

DRIVERS RIVER

drain the eastern slopes. Blue Mountain streams, especially at higher altitudes, are cool, clear and turbulent. At upstream sites, small streams and rivulets flow through deeply incised, steep-sided gorges and are relatively inaccessible except where they cross tracks and trails. In the lower reaches, the valleys are flat and broad. Most Blue Mountain streams are perennial except under extreme drought conditions. However, because of diversions from the Yallahs and Hope Rivers, the lower watercourses of these rivers are more often than not quite dry.

RIO GRANDE

In addition to their value as resources for human use, mountain rivers and streams are important reservoirs of biodiversity, from the unostentatious mosses and algae encrusting the rocks to the more spectacular shrimp and fish. A look under the rocks and among the plants in the stream channel would reveal several animals swimming and crawling towards hiding places. Admittedly, many of these animals are small and easily unnoticed, but they form an important part of the biological resources.

Research carried out in the Blue Mountain streams by Kimberly John and Eric Hyslop shows that the most diverse group of animals present is the insects. Many of these spend their larval and nymphal stages in water. The relatively large predatory nymphs of dragonflies and damselflies are fully adapted to aquatic life. Their mask-like mouthparts can be extended outwards to capture prey. Adult caddisflies look like hairy moths, but the small larvae (up to 1.5 cm – half an inch – long) are 100 per cent aquatic. Some caddisfly larvae, like the endemic hydropschid (*Smicridea jamaicensis*) live freely in the water current and construct nets of silk that trap food particles. The food-enriched net is then eaten. Other caddisfly larvae are case-bearing and are camouflaged in helical, cap-shaped, tubular or flat cases

DRAGONFLY NYMPH

DRAGONFLY

Guide to the Blue and John Crow Mountains

Life in the Streams and Rivers

WHIRLIGIG BEETLE

JANGA

composed of tiny stones, leaves and other plant debris. Mayflies spend most of their lives as small (0.5 to 1 cm), delicate nymphs in the streams. The winged adults seldom feed. Most live just long enough to mate and lay eggs, from a few hours to a couple of days.

Other insects are only semi-aquatic. Among these, you might encounter diving beetles and whirligigs – which, as the name suggests, whirl around on the surface of pools. These should not be confused with the water bugs, which may dive like the rapacious Belostomatids or skate over the water surface like the pond-skaters.

Most of the snails in the Blue Mountains are small. The live-bearing Thiarids grow up to 4 cm (1.5 in) long and, in some situations, achieve high densities. The Physid snails are also small, reaching a maximum of 1 cm (0.3 in) in length. However, the Bussu snail has achieved some human recognition as the chief ingredient in Bussu soup from the streams of Portland.

The crustaceans of the Blue Mountain streams are well known, not only because of their relatively large sizes but also by virtue of their culinary potential. In the cool, clear high-altitude streams one can find an abundance of small Grapsid crabs (up to 4 cm – 1.5 in wide). These are primarily scavengers. The larger streams and rivers, however, are home to two families of freshwater shrimp (both locally called 'janga'), the more common

BUSSU SHELLS

191

being the *Palaemonid Machrobrachium* sp. Both families migrate up and down the rivers as part of their natural life cycle. The freshwater shrimp are nocturnal and are rarely seen during the day, unless their hiding places under rocks and leaf litter are disturbed. They are spear-hunted at night by local people or caught in special traps.

Since Jamaica is geologically relatively young and a small island, its native freshwater fish fauna is poor, being dominated by the relatives of marine species that have adapted to stream conditions. Among these are the mullets, the sleepers, and the gobies (locally called 'suckstone'). The mountain mullet is found primarily in the high-altitude streams of the Blue Mountains and is popular in recreational fishing. It has been suggested that the mullets still spawn in the sea, or that at least their early life is spent in the marine environment. Some of the gobies also require seawater in the early life stages. Gobies and sleepers are small fish, up to 4 cm (1.5 in) long, which swim close to or even crawl along the streambeds. Although scarce, they may be found throughout Blue Mountain streams.

Among the truly freshwater fish in the streams are the four species of small fish belonging to the family Poecilidae. Two species are native: the tiki-tiki or *Gambusia* and the *Limia*. The other poecilids are ornamentals: the swordtails were introduced from Mexico, and the colourful guppies from Trinidad. Two species of African perch *(Tilapia)* were introduced from outside of Jamaica. Originally from southeast and west Africa respectively, *Oreochromis mossambica* and *O. niloticus* have established themselves in the middle to lower reaches of Blue Mountain streams and have become important in subsistence fishing.

APPENDIX

GENERAL INFORMATION

The following members of the Natural History Society of Jamaica, having explored the Blue and John Crow Mountains for this guidebook, may be available for updates, information and guiding (all Jamaica telephone numbers have the area code 876):

Hermann Tobisch
Tel: 702-2888
Email: catja@jamweb.com

Jill Byles
Tel 977-8007
Email paraisoj@cwjamaica.com

OTHER RESOURCES

Natural History Society of Jamaica (NHSJ)
Department of Life Sciences, UWI, Mona, Kingston 7
Tel: 927-1202
Fax: 977-1035
Email: nhsj@uwimona.edu.jm

Jamaica Conservation and Development Trust (JCDT), **National Park Management**
29 Dumbarton Avenue, Kingston 10
Tel: 876-920-8278, 876-920-8279, 876-960-2848–9
Fax: 876-960-2850
Email: jcdt@jcdt.org
Website: http//:jcdt.org

For information on accommodation and bookings at Holywell and Portland Gap also fees, possible guides, blocked roads and emergencies in the Blue Mountain Peak area, contact the JCDT above.

For general emergencies such as car accidents, phone the police on 119.

For weather conditions, phone the Meteorological Office, tel: 929-3694, 929-3700, 929-3706 or 116.

TOUR COMPANIES

These companies arrange for tour guides and accommodation when necessary.

HERITAGE TOURS

Ainsley Henriques
Tel: 759-7804
Website: www.heritageja.com
Fax: 938-2578
Email: heritagetoursja@cwjamaica.com

Tours from Bath, St. Thomas, to Corn Puss Gap and Millbank, Portland (also boat trips to Pigeon Island).

SUNVENTURE TOURS

Robert Kerr
Tel: 960-6685
Website: www.sunventuretours.com

Tours for nature lovers, camping, hiking, cycling (Robert Kerr wrote the introduction to this guidebook).

VALLEY HIKES

P.O. Box 89, Port Antonio, Portland
Tel: 993-3881

Valley Hikes is a non-governmental organisation (NGO) whose governing board includes representatives from the Jamaica Tourist Board, the National Park, the local environmental association and the Rio Grande Valley project. It arranges guides and accommodation in the Rio Grande area when needed.

COUNTRYSTYLE INTERNATIONAL LTD

Diana McIntyre-Pike
Tel: 1-340-6176, or

Barry Bonitto
Tel: 962-7758
Email: Countrystyle@mail.infochan.com

Operating from Mandeville, Unique Jamaica Countrystyle Community offers tours which include farms in the Mavis Bank area and to Holywell Nature Reserve, and also guided hiking.

BIRDWATCHING

Those especially interested in birdwatching should contact Bird Life Jamaica on Mondays, Wednesdays or Fridays between 9 a.m. and 4 p.m., tel: 927-1864, email birdlifejamaica@yahoo.com. Other useful contact numbers include:

- **Forres Park**, birdwatching in coffee country
  Tel: 927-8275

- **John Fletcher of Bird Life Jamaica**
  Tel: 931-4205
  Email: coffee@kasnet.com

- **Ryan Love**
  Email: ryanlove2k3@yahoo.com

- **Mocking Bird Hill Hotel**, Port Antonio
  Tel: 993-7267, 993-9134,
  Email:birdees@mail.infochan.com,
  Website: www.hotelmockingbirdhill.com

LOCAL GUIDES

In Jacks Hill, the foothills between Kingston and the Mammee River, a local guide is Tony Mitchell, tel: 702-0143, who lives beside the shop in Jacks Hill.

There are numerous trails, now largely disused, between Jacks Hill and the Mammee River, which run along by Maryland and Woodford and up the slopes to the Newcastle road and Holywell.

In Mavis Bank, for reliable guides to the Peak via Penlyne Castle and its surroundings, contact Joyce Bennett on 977-8360. She also has available accommodation at Mavis Bank Top Road.

At Guava Ridge, for the surrounding area, call Lynford Sterling at 1-458-4221.

ACCOMMODATION

The Jamaica Tourist Board has a list of all the major hotels, villas and cottages to rent, which it inspects to see that its standards are upheld. These are mostly on the coast or in tourist centres. Very few are within easy reach of the BMJC National Park and surroundings, with the exception of the Strawberry Hill Hotel on the Newcastle road and the Mocking Bird Hill Hotel in Portland.

Some of the following accommodations may not be on the JTB list, and we can take no responsibility for standards. They are listed because they have been used by travellers to the mountains, and some are very affordable. They vary from comfortable cottages to floor or tent space.

BLUE MOUNTAIN AREA

STRAWBERRY HILL HOTEL

On a hilltop above Irish Town on the Newcastle road. Beautiful but expensive. Tel: 944-8400 or 944-8409. Web site: www.islandoutpost.com/strawberry_hill/

ANDREW AND LISA GORDON

Offer Bed and Breakfast at a rural cottage off Dustry road. This runs between Newcastle road and Maryland. Tel: 944 8394 for further information.

HERITAGE GARDENS OF COLD SPRING

Near Newcastle. Gardens, cottage for rent. Proprietor, Ms Eleanor Jones, tel: 960-0974 or 929-9481.

TREE TOPS

A two-bedroom cottage beside Heritage Gardens. Email: bluejamaica@kasnet.com.

THE GAP CAFÉ AND GIFT SHOP

Also has accommodation, apartment with bedroom, two single beds, bathroom, living room and verandah, B&B. Proprietor, Ms Gloria Palomino, tel: 997-3032 or 923-7078.

HOLYWELL CABINS

There are three log cabins for rent in Holywell, run by Jamaica Conservation and Development Trust, tel: 920-8278–9, 960-2848–9, email: jcdt@jcdt.org

Rates, park entrance: locals – adults J$100, children J$50; visitors – adults US$5, children US$2. Two cabins sleep four and one sleeps six, and both tent sites and tents are available.

STARLIGHT CHALET AND HEALTH SPA

At Silver Hill Gap. One-, two-, and three-bedroom suites with kitchens. Meals available by arrangement. Tel: 969-3116 or 906-3075, fax: 969-5129, website: <www.starlightchalet.com>, email: chalet@cwjamaica.com.

WILD FLOWER LODGE

Near Penlyne Castle and Blue Mountain trail. Accommodation consists of 42 bunk beds in dormitories, two private rooms with two beds each and one cottage with two bedrooms. Meals provided by arrangement. Lighting by kerosene lamps. Transport to and from Mavis Bank and guides by arrangement. Proprietor, Mr Eric Lieba, tel: 1-364-0722.

WHITFIELD HALL HOSTEL AND FARM

Near Blue Mountain trail. Dormitory accommodation for 13 people. Separate two-bedroom cottages for eight people. Cooking facilities, meals by special arrangement. Kerosene lighting. Tel: 927-0986.

FORRES PARK

Near Mavis Bank. Main house and cabins, US$60 per night, meals extra. Accommodation can also be arranged at Abbey Green at the foot of Blue Mountain trail, and transport to and from for those wishing to climb the Peak. Tel: 927-8275.

LIMETREE FARM

Beyond Tower Hill. Road starts beside Mavis Bank Central factory. Three cabins in scenic setting. Meals and transport available. Tel: 887-8788. website:limetreefarm.com. Email: hello@limetreefarm.com

MAVIS BANK BED & BREAKFAST.

Accommodation for four. Proprietor, Joyce Bennett, tel: 977-8161.
Scorpion Inn: a large establishment overlooking the road between Mavis Bank and Mt. Charles. Tel: 944-7912-3.

BLUE MOUNTAIN TRAIL, ACCOMMODATION AT PORTLAND GAP

Supervised by National Park rangers, this is a pleasantly landscaped area to the side of the trail at Portland Gap. Wooden cabins, toilets and cooking facilities are provided in a garden atmosphere, blending into the natural environment. There is an entrance fee. Accommodation includes five rooms sleeping between 12 and 20 persons in bunks or on the floor. Tent space is available and tents and foam mattresses can be rented if required. Barbecues are provided, and there is a tuck shop. Bring your own cooking pots and food. Tel: JCDT (see page 194).

ST. MARY

TAPIOCA VILLAGE RETREAT, DEVON PEN

B&B, cabins and camping. Tel: 922-2341, 1-369-8218, 1-341-6215, email: tfc-catering@infochan.com.

RIVER'S EDGE, NEAR ANNOTTO BAY

Dormitory and two suites sleeping 45. Catering available for large groups. Tel: 944-2673, email: riveredge99@hotmail.com.

NATURE'S PLACE

West of the Spanish River Bridge on the north coast highway, a well kept property can be let for special events or camping. Tents available. Contact Mr F. White. Tel: 926-6765.

ST. THOMAS

FOUNTAIN HOTEL

An old spa hotel based on the Bath mineral springs, with rooms to rent and hot spring baths. Tel: 703-4345 or 703-4154.

PROSPECT

There are guesthouses and cottages for rent along the coast, particularly at Long Bay and Prospect. Daphne Lewis rents beach cottages, email: lewiscraft@cwjamaica.com

THE JOHN CROW MOUNTAINS AND RIO GRANDE VALLEY

BOWDEN PEN

Access from Bath via Corn Puss Gap trail, or from Hayfield via Cuna Cuna Pass trail, or from Portland via Millbank. A real country experience. Bowden Pen sits on the St. Thomas side of the mountain ridge dividing St. Thomas and Portland, with a waterfall and mountain stream nearby. Accommodation includes 25 cottages, most with two double beds, some with more, some with floorspace and mattresses and bedding, one housing 25 people. Chemical toilets and showers. Meals by arrangement, traditional food cooked in the traditional way. Proprietor, Ms Linette Wilks, tel: 1-395-5351.

PORTLAND

There are numerous hotels, villas and apartments in Port Antonio along the north and northeast coast, and some inland. They vary enormously in quality and price. Up-to-date information and advice can be obtained from Valley Hikes in Port Antonio, tel: 993-3881. The Jamaica Tourist Board Centre, also in Port Antonio, may also be helpful in locating accommodation. It is located at City Plaza, tel: 993-3051, 993-2587.

MOCKING BIRD HILL HOTEL

A boutique hotel which has won awards for environmentally friendly practices. It promotes ecotourism, particularly birdwatching. Tel: 993-7267 or 993-7134, fax: 993-7133, email: birdees@mail.infochan.com.

BLUEBERRY HILL GUEST HOUSE, KILDARE, BUFF BAY

Convenient for hiking the Buff Bay Valley. Tel: 913-6814.

FOOD AND DRINK

WAYSIDE SHOPS AND BARS

These are numerous on main roads, selling soft drinks and beers. Often they sell crisps, biscuits and sometimes bullas and other food. There are also itinerant vendors of fruits and homemade sweetmeats. Fresh coconut water is the most refreshing of drinks. Mangos, bananas, naseberries and other fruits are available according to season.

CAFÉS, RESTAURANTS AND HOTELS

There are several local fast food outlets on the Junction road at Devon Pen. River's Edge, near Annotto Bay, will cater meals for small and large groups by prior arrangement – tel: 944-2673, email: riveredge99@hotmail.com. Boston Bay jerk pork stands are known island-wide for their appetising jerked meats, served with roasted breadfruit. Most of the larger towns in Jamaica – for example, Morant Bay, Buff Bay, and Port Antonio – have cafés. Port Antonio has some excellent cafés and affordable hotels. Long Bay has two popular good beach resturants and bars.

CRYSTAL EDGE

On the Newcastle road at Irish town. A good meal can be had at a reasonable price.
A new coffee shop, Café Blue, is next door, selling coffee and cake.

STRAWBERRY HILL HOTEL AND SPA

Strawberry Hill is a little above Irish Town. It offers a wonderful brunch at weekends. Telephone in advance for rates and bookings, 944-8400 or 944-8408.

THE GAP CAFÉ

Between Newcastle and Holywell; coffee and meals by prior arrangement except weekends. To book, tel: 1-997-3032 or 923-7078.

STARLIGHT CHALET AND HEALTH SPA

This small hotel, which serves meals by prior arrangement, is situated at Silver Hill Gap. To reach it, continue along the road, turning into Portland at the Holywell entrance, bearing right instead of turning left to Buff Bay, and on to the hotel, where the road turns sharply downhill. The drive into the chalet is at the corner. Tel: 969-3116 or 985-9830.

FORRES PARK

Near Mavis Bank. Meals by prior arrangement, tel: 927-8275.

TAPIOCA VILLAGE RETREAT, DEVON PEN, ST. MARY

It is best to book ahead. Tel: 922-2341, 1-369-8218 or 1-341-6215, email: tfc-catering@infochan.com.

TRANSPORT

Country buses run from Kingston; from Papine to Mavis Bank; from Constant Spring at the end of the Constant Spring Road to Golden Spring, Castleton and Annotto Bay; and from East Queens Street, near Parade in Kingston, to St. Thomas.

Minibuses and taxis are also numerous on these routes. Beware of loud music and fast driving. The red-plated ones are registered and therefore legal and carry passenger insurance.

Excursion buses can be hired by parties to take them to and from where they want to go.

For rental cars and excursion buses, see the Yellow Pages of the telephone directory. 4WD cars with drivers can be arranged for some areas – for example, Mavis Bank to Hagley Gap on the way to Blue Mountain Peak. Owners of accommodations in the area will arrange transport for guests: Whitfield Hall, tel: 876-927-0986; Wild Flower Lodge, tel: 1-364-0722; and Forres Park, from Mavis Bank to Abbey Green, tel: 927-8275.

SPECIAL ATTRACTIONS

Bath Botanical Gardens, St. Thomas

Bath Fountain, on hot mineral springs
Tel: 703-4345, 703-4154

Castleton Botanic Gardens, Junction Road, St. Mary
Catherine's Peak

Charles Town Maroon Museum near Buff Bay
Tel: Frank Lumsden 1-445-2861

Cinchona Botanic Gardens

Downhill cycling, Blue Mountain Bicycle Tours Ltd
Tel: 974 7075

Heritage Gardens of Cold Spring
Tel: 960-0794

Holywell Nature Reserve
Tel: 920-8278, 920-8279, 960-2848–9

Holywell spring festival Misty Bliss in February or March

Hope Botanical Gardens, Hope Road, Kingston

Mavis Bank Central Coffee Factory tour
Tel: 977-8005

Moore Town: Nanny Monument and Museum

Newcastle Parade Ground

Rafter's Rest for Rio Grande rafting
Tel: 993-5163 / 993-5778

Reach Falls, near Reach, Portland

River's Edge, on the Pencar River near Annotto Bay
Tel: 944-2673

Somerset Falls, between Hope Bay and St. Margaret's Bay

Ueshima Coffee Farm and Great House, Craigton
Tel: 944-8653, 929-8490-1

White River Pools, Craigmill, St. Mary

White River Falls, near Millbank, Portland

Check newspapers, go-jamaica.com, or whatsonjamaica.com for local festivals, dates and locations.

THE NATURAL HISTORY SOCIETY OF JAMAICA

The Natural History Society of Jamaica is a non-profit, non-governmental organization which was formed in 1940 by scientists and teachers across the island. At that time little was known or taught about our natural history.

Our purpose now, as then, is to study and disseminate information about Jamaica's bio-diversity and promote conservation of our wild life and natural habitats.

Our main activites are field trips and lectures, production of a monthly news sheet, educational work with schools, and socially, an annual lunch for the society. To find out more or join the society write or phone:

The Natural History Society of Jamaica
C/O Department of Life Sciences
The University of the West Indies
Mona, Kingston 7, Jamaica
Tel: (876) 977-6938; Fax: (876) 977-1075
Email: naturalhistory@hotmail.com